SEEING LESSONS

SEEING LESSONS

14 Life Secrets
I've Learned Along the Way

TOM SULLIVAN

WILEY

John Wiley & Sons, Inc.

Published by John Wiley & Sons, Inc., Hoboken, New Jersey
Published simultaneously in Canada

Design and production by Navta Associates, Inc.

The author gratefully acknowledges the following for permission to quote from *Journey through Heartsong* by Mattie J. T. Stepanek. Copyright © 2001 Mattie Stepanek. Reprinted by permission of Hyperion and VSP Books. The author also thanks Beth Rothenberg for her lecture on creating a life plan.

For general information about our other products and services, please contact our Customer Care Department within the United States at (800) 762-2974, outside the United States at (317) 572-3993 or fax (317) 572-4002.

Wiley also publishes its books in a variety of electronic formats. Some content that appears in print may not be available in electronic books. For more information about Wiley products, visit our web site at www.wiley.com.

Library of Congress Cataloging-in-Publication Data:
Sullivan, Tom, date.
   Seeing lessons : 14 life secrets I've learned along the way / Tom Sullivan.
     p. cm.
   ISBN 0-471-26356-7
   1. Sullivan, Tom, 1947- 2. Blind–United States–Biography. 3. Blind musicians–United States–Biography. 4. Conduct of life. 5. Self-actualization (Psychology) I. Title.
   HV1792.S85A3 2003
362.4'1'092–dc21   2003002421

Printed in the United States of America

10 9 8 7 6 5 4 3 2 1

To Patty, who taught me to see life's most important lesson:
to love unconditionally.

CONTENTS

CONTENTS

CONTENTS

ACKNOWLEDGMENTS

To all of the people whose stories are contained in these pages—you have been may teachers, friends, and inspiration as I work to see life with the clarity of inner vision.

To my agent, Bob Diforio, thank you for fighting the good fight, pal, and finding the outlet for these lessons to see the light of day.

To all of the folks at EDA, most notably Marge, for impeccable reading and commitment to all of my creative work; Mabel, who defies age with her enthusiasm and passion; and most especially to my friend Alex, who labored with me over writing and rewriting with joy and candor when I got off track.

To my editor, Tom Miller, thanks for not letting my stories run too long, and, most important, thank you for always editing while listening to the sound of my voice.

SEEING LESSONS

PROLOGUE

The ballroom of the New York Marriott was full. A number of the city's most influential people, along with my family and friends, had put on formal wear and come to celebrate the Helen Keller American Foundation for the Blind Lifetime Achievement Award, given only twice in the eighty-year history of the organization. As I stood under the glare of the spotlight and listened to the master of ceremonies wax eloquently over my accomplishments, I found myself wondering seriously, Why? What had I done that would be considered special or remarkable? Had I really made a difference in the lives of others? Or, had I been just an anomaly, an oddity to those with sight, a blind person who had lived his life as a risk-taker? Was I blind first or a person that happened to be blind? I was fifty years old, and it seemed odd to be asking these questions. But I suppose we all arrive at crossroads of reflection, and if we're going to grow, these moments are necessary.

I understood that at my core I wanted to be a contributor to the common good. Were my achievements tangible enough to serve a purpose, or did they just make for good press? Who benefited because I could hit a golf ball well or ski fast, run marathons, or even sing well? My writings had been principally about me, a rather boring subject after all these years. Had I said anything that was more than just a sound bite? Balancing the life scale, I knew I'd been a good father and husband; I believed I was a friend others could count on, and looking back under the glare of the spotlight, I was comfortable in the knowledge that for the most part I had followed the old rule and treated others the way I wanted to be treated. Fine. But what would be my legacy? How would people benefit from the fact that I had been here? At that moment on the stage in front of three thousand well-dressed and well-heeled patrons, it dawned on me that my life needed to be about ideas. What I left behind would be measured by my ability to articulate my perceptions into life lessons that would be tangible to others. What were the real life lessons that could be drawn from a life without sight?

That night back in our suite, after all the hoopla, my wife, Patty, and I sat on the couch sharing a glass of wine in the quiet comfort reserved only for couples whose love has deepened over many years. The concept of one true love is not new, but the fact that we have adapted and enriched our love through a complex set of circumstances brought about by my blindness is unique and central to our life. Each of us is more than we might have been due to the other's perspective and sensitivity. For example, while I've exposed Patty to the richness of the senses, she has filled in the gaps for a husband without eyes.

I couldn't help but become excited as my mind began to explore other facets of a life in the dark. In this epiphany of awareness, I understood that I was privileged to possess a different kind of vision. Over the last fifteen years, I had lectured at more than two thousand colleges and corporations around the world, synthesizing my thoughts into what I hoped were memorable quotes. But a speech is a performance in which the audience is affected as much by how you say things as the words themselves.

I took stock of the inventory found in the ideas that had become the signature pieces of my lectures. I often talk about the senses as our antennae on the world. All of us possess the ability—no, the unlimited possibility—of sharpening our sensory acuity. It really is a question of wanting to. Why not taste a snowflake on a winter day; enjoy the first smell of the ground as it opens, announcing the coming of spring; feel the pull of a trout on a line; and listen to the sound of a stream rolling over century-worn pebbles? The pot-pourri of information acquired by the senses is infinite. I considered how much we could learn about each other beyond the visual.

Have you ever taken the time to listen to the sound of a smile or examined the type of personality represented in the way we per-form the simple act of shaking hands? How we say things can teach us as much about real feelings as what is actually said. And then there's all the nuance that goes with a sigh or the rhythm in a per-son's breathing. Consider vocal intonation or even stuttering; there's so much to know.

It's said that beauty is only skin deep, and I believe in this pro-found truth. I know Patty is extremely beautiful, but it's the inside out of her beauty that will continue to make me love her forever. I've never met an ugly person—unless that person wanted to be ugly—in other words, what he or she reflected to others was ugliness. I understand that I carry no predisposition to label anyone. I've never had to deal with a prejudice based on a physical characteristic—for example, the color of a person's skin or an obvious oddity in appear-ance. Being an optimist, I've been able to meet people always with the hope that I will find basic goodness, integrity, and character. But I'm not a Pollyanna; I've endured prejudice all my life. Even now, the stereotypes that go with being blind still linger.

· · ·

3

Earlier in the evening, the server responsible for the head table asked Patty what I would like to eat rather than speaking to me directly.

People often make assumptions about my other senses. I'm amazed that many people still believe that extraordinary hearing goes along with the label "blind." The fact is, it's just a necessary compensation. Recently, I had to listen to a man's comment as if it were a statement of fact: that all people without sight are great musicians. Let me tell you, there are a lot of tone-deaf blind folks out there.

And, there are still prejudices in the job place. I've been denied work on certain television shows or in film because either being blind was considered detrimental to the role or it was thought of as a label the public couldn't look past in accepting the character I might play. Probably the worst snub of all is when a sighted actor is placed in a part that obviously was written for a competent artist with a disability. I yearn for the day when I will get the chance to act in a project in which being blind is not even mentioned as a part of the story.

I had to admit that I was still working to improve my capacity at reading where people were really coming from when dealing with my label. I had made the decision a long time ago that ignorance is much more acceptable than attitude and that I must spend my life as a teacher if we're ever going to rise above the predisposition that comes with stereotyping.

As it does so often at night, my mind jumped to another subject and I found myself thinking about my mother. She would have loved being here on this grand evening, but she had been taken from us by the ravages of cancer a few years ago. In the last four months of her life, I shared the caregiving responsibilities with my sisters, and for the first time this very guarded Irish Catholic woman expressed her true feelings on subjects ranging from the pain of a broken marriage to her anguish and thoughts of suicide when she learned that I was blind.

She spoke of her childhood, growing up in the tenements of Boston, and her deeply held belief that God was the supreme being and would soon bring her home. There was a beauty in her death and a perfect completion to the circle of her life. Although her loss was profound for all of us, clearly we could find positives even in her death.

This fundamental concept of turning disadvantage into advantage is one of my most important life lessons. Even in this life passage, the pain and trauma of loss became an advantage with the renewal of relationship lost for so long with my sisters, and, more important, the treasures my mother revealed to all of us over those last days.

My sisters and I live on opposite coasts, so we do not see each other often. We are far apart in age. Peggy is seven years older than I am, and Jean precedes me by fifteen years. It wasn't until we worked together caring for our mother, sharing in the common purpose of loving her, that we came to understand how much we really cared for one another. I was struck by the idea that we all wish we could hold on to meaningful moments in our lives—those singularly important experiences that change and define us.

A major life lesson for me deals with recognizing significant turning points in our development. The ability to rise to the occasion and bring our best concentration and application to the moment separates those of us who drink deep from the cup of life from those who are just passengers on the train.

I couldn't help remembering another important element in the makeup of Tom Sullivan: the search for a positive self-image. None of us see ourselves as others see us, and our feelings of self-worth are greatly affected by the opinions of others. As a child, I faced the ridicule and cruelty of other children. Only through discovering the strength released by my competitive anger was I able to find talents in music, academics, and sports, that allowed me to celebrate my uniqueness. Self-worth comes about by having a dream, taking a risk, and doing the work. Only through failure can success take on real meaning.

As often happens in the wee hours, the free association of ideas came tumbling out of my head. I found that I was considering the four p's of my philosophy: pride, people, purpose, and passion. I define pride as personal responsibility for individual daily effort, and I believe that none of us can grow without demonstrating commitment to our personal responsibility. Like many of us, I'm very concerned that we have become a selfish, not a selfless society. We seem to have lost our way when demonstrating individual daily effort on behalf of public service or social programs. And as the level of selfishness increases, our ability to connect to people declines.

Each of us needs to define a personal vision statement that keeps us purposeful. My vision statement reflects this commitment to purpose: I live to be the best Tom Sullivan possible. I intend to make a difference in the lives of everyone I touch by gaining from their knowledge and enriching my own experience, sharing the best of who I am with every person I meet. I *will* change the stereotype so that someday I will be known as a man who happened to be blind, rather than a blind man. I will turn my disability into an ability. And how will I achieve such lofty goals? By expressing all activities of my life with absolute passion. Passion is the catalyst, the zing, the thing that all of us must apply to our lives if we're going to fulfill our hopes, dreams, aspirations, and desires.

The most important gift Patty has given me is that through her love I have recognized the balance between independence, dependence, and interdependence. When I was a child, the world categorized me as dependent. I spent my early life trying desperately to prove that I was independent. I raged at windmills, constantly defying the odds and struggling to assert my right to freedom. No risk was too great, no challenge impossible. But behind the extreme behavior was a person needing to be loved. Patty's extraordinary ability to love unconditionally created a level of trust that allowed me to share a life of interdependence. It is my formula for true happiness.

This book is an eclectic composite of life experiences molded into a philosophy that I hope you'll find useful. Frankly, as I see it, life is as good as life gets. I know that I am much more valuable as a blind person than I ever would have been had I been given the gift of sight. As I write this work, I hope to provide you with a little knowledge, a touch of motivation, a dash of perspective, and a whole lot of inspiration.

Live Your Life with All Your Common Senses

The senses serve as entrances to an inner world. Not the senses I have but what I do with them is my kingdom.
—Helen Keller

Be Completely Aware

I confirm that I'm alive when my senses inform me that it's the start of a new day. Sometimes sound is the messenger sense. I'm often aware before I'm completely awake of the cheery good morning sung by a robin in the large oak tree at the far corner of my yard. His ebullient expression of natural joy suggests that he has just eaten the proverbial worm and that all is right with heaven and earth.

My wife, Patricia, still slumbers peacefully. Her rhythmic breathing tells me she'll sleep in for another hour. I wonder what she's dreaming about. I take in her smell. It is all love. All woman. All life.

A Marvelous Run

My dog Partner and I will soon be sharing a run along my Palos Verdes, California, beach. It is *my* beach—at least I like to think so. I figure that no one could possibly be more appreciative of its sensory secrets than I am. There is a magical renewal of the spirit every day I run along this marvelous confluence of land and ocean.

I hear the tingling of metal from beside my bed as my German shepherd guide dog recognizes that I'm awake. Rising from his spot on the floor, he licks my outstretched hand as if to say, "Good morning, Master." He, too, knows it's time to run. It's his happiest experience, and we share it passionately. It's early June, but if the feeling's right, we might end our exercise with a cold swim in the Pacific. Ten years ago that wouldn't have even been a question. I would've launched into the chilly ocean water with a bravado reserved for youth. Now in my fifties, I'm finding that I'm beginning to pick my spots and not always challenge the ocean's cold.

I define the intersecting of the senses as the ultimate harmony. It is seamless and beautiful. No musical chord could ever express such total richness and balance. No painting could ever reflect its perfection. Feeling it, living it, knowing it—this harmony has made the disability of my blindness not only tolerable but joyous.

This time of year, the smell spectrum is superb, from mock orange blossoms to jasmine, eucalyptus to roses. I am assaulted with an abundance of olfactory stimulation. Songbirds blend with seagulls' cries, and the dissonant cacophony is wonderful to hear. I call this *syntonicity*—being in tune with the nature around me, the natural order of things entering my brain through every sensory antennae.

The air is misty with the early morning fog, and the ground reflects the moisture as I touch fallen leaves that are slippery under my feet. The dog is so careful; he never rushes. I smell the ocean before I hear its sound. The wind blows southwest off the Pacific, and there's a long hill that leads down from the road to the sand. The ocean's smell funnels up this hill and reaches me a half mile before I arrive at the bluff. I love the taste of the Pacific, including most of the stuff that swims in it. It touches my tongue and tastes old, salty, and clean. Now Partner can't help himself. He picks up the pace, and we are almost jogging. I hear the first sound of the immense power of the surf as it blocks out the bird song. It's an odd experience because it closes out most of the rest of my audio capacity. I love it, but in some ways I'm afraid of it. I am now completely dependent on my big dog and the messages he sends through the harness.

There are fifteen different kinds of waves that caress and bombard the California coast. I've come to know them all. At low tide, the sound reminds me of the wind blowing through buffalo grass somewhere on the plains of rural Nebraska. It roars over the sand dunes, arching across the complete audio spectrum as it follows the curvature of the coast. It seems to never run out of energy, and I have the impression that at any moment it could gobble up the land. When the tide is high, the sound is very different. I am reminded of a prizefight as the incoming waves punch the outgoing sand with a powerful thud in a round-by-round confrontation that never ends.

I love it when the sea is flattened by the sky. In winter, rain pounds the surf into sublime submission. My impression is that there must be a Higher Power still calling the shots. At least I like to think so.

This morning the waves are at ten- to twelve-second intervals. On other days, when the chop is up and white caps dot the horizon, the interval can be as little as three seconds, and the sound reminds me of small-arms fire. No morning sounds the same on the beach, with the waves painting a portrait in sound, rich colors that a blind person can truly appreciate. With the tide out, the kelp clinging to the rocks at the far end of this spit of sand is full of life. The smell speaks to the whole cycle of creation. I can smell new plankton and life lost during the last high tide. *Holostheiae*, the Greeks say—heart, mind, soul, and body—all of it connected in a sensory collage.

I run with Partner as hard as I can. I am exhausted but exhilarated, removing the dog's harness and my shoes quickly as we dash with a whoop into the ocean, diving under the surf. My head is chilled by the cold, but I love it. I swim straight out, probably two hundred yards beyond the surf line, beyond sound.

Rolling onto my back, I allow myself to be rocked by the ocean's swell, knowing that I am completely safe. Partner breathes next to me, and I am sure that he understands exactly how to navigate us home. I'm not thinking out here, not planning my day or worrying about the future. I am at peace.

We remain this way for a few minutes, then reluctantly I place my hand on the neck of my friend, allowing him to swim us in. As my feet touch the ground and I work my way onto the shore, Partner shakes the water from his fur and again touches me with his head. The dog knows the drill. I take his collar, and he helps me find the discarded shirt, shoes, harness, and leash. It's been a perfect start to what promises to be a perfect day. Nothing in creation is as connected and seamless as the way in which our senses gather information, send it in a nanosecond to the brain, and inculcate it into a common sense awareness.

The Synergy of the Senses

I define sensory synergism as the perfect coming together of data gathered through our sensory antennae and collated by the brain into a recognizable experience, thought, or impression. We are ultimately alive at these special moments, and when they occur, we always remember them. Athletes describe it as being in the zone. Musicians define it as grooving, in the pocket, solid. Artists can't wait to translate the palette of the mind to the palette of the canvas, and those who meditate frame it as a clear channel experience. On the other hand, scientists talk about carrying on mental processing of sensory information somewhere in the cerebral cortex, and even more complex elements that take us into the area of brain synapses or sensory operational modalities—all extremely interesting but not helpful in furthering our personal access to the joy of sensory synergism.

Of course, I would like to see the world in the way that a person with sight does, yet I would not trade my life connection with the senses for even the most beautiful sunset. I've come to accept the premise that sight is the lead sense and most people gain information through visual recognition as your primary tool in order to understand the world. The other senses take on the role of supporting cast as in a play or film. People often tell me that they could not possibly imagine what it must be like to be blind and that the onset of blindness would be the hardest loss of any of the five senses to bear.

Helen Keller disagreed. She gave us the most introspective insight into this remarkably complex issue. When asked late in her life what sensory loss she would deem as the most debilitating, she immediately spoke to the issue of sound. She said, "It is in sound that fundamental communication finds its essence, and human beings gain their greatest understanding of another's attitudes and feelings."

The possibilities for sensory growth are virtually unlimited, and I hope that you're anxious to begin experimenting with your own sensory development. We have the capacity to either isolate each sensory stimulus individually or combine them collectively. When you rely primarily on sight and disregard the effectiveness of the other members of your sensory team, you're like Shaquille O'Neal without Kobe Bryant of the L.A. Lakers or like a conductor without an orchestra.

How do the senses plug into our recognition and evaluation of each other? Have you ever recognized the personal scent of your mate in a crowd? Every one of us has a distinct and individual voiceprint just as unique as the visual differences in our appearance. Shaking hands with a stranger projects as much about him or her as a fingerprint on file with the FBI.

Since sight is the dominant sense, it is easy for people to make immediate visual judgments about one another. Blindness has allowed me to step back and appreciate the coming together of four glorious senses. I have treasured the opportunity to personally evaluate and understand every human being I meet. The true and effective use of instinct occurs when our brain's remarkable computer receives feedback from all of the senses. Our ability to make instant judgments is immensely enhanced when the data are gathered from every sensory outlet rather than just our visual center.

Being blind creates an extraordinary psychological and sensory dynamic, particularly when I meet people for the first time. Right from the initial handshake, I know exactly where they're coming from. Is the first touch dynamic? If it is, generally the shake is firm and it lasts a beat while we complete some form of basic human connection. Then there are the pumpers. These people are generally insincere and carry on an exaggerated up-and-down motion to avoid intimacy. The fingertip shake—when two hands don't actually interlock because the other person only presents you with his or her fingers—suggests superiority. The worst of all is the handshake of the wimp—the person with no obvious dynamics who just barely makes civil contact.

These dynamics are further developed in my case because of many people's discomfort when first meeting a blind person. At the same time their palm is sweating and their eyes are looking away, they tend to be speaking with an exaggerated volume level, as if I must not only be blind but deaf. In these moments of discomfort, I am compelled to try to put people at ease, so usually I place my left hand over our two hands in a gesture of warmth and friendship. I know I've lost any possibility of connection when the other person flinches and pulls his or her hand away.

Extending the handshake to the next level, a hug says it all. Is it a hug of friendship or a hug of sexual intent? Is it a hug saying I love you or a hug asking you to love me? Is it a cursory slap on the back or a massage of emotional commitment? Is it an upper body lean that says keep your distance or a full body embrace that speaks to a commitment? If the handshake is a dynamic sensory imprint, a hug stands as the defining statement of human intent.

Have you observed that when people are under stress you can smell the toxins they excrete? Their odor is filled with tension that hangs suspended in the air all around them, and if you're a true sensory observer, whether it's in your own family dynamic or a corporate meeting, you can be way ahead of the game by letting your olfactory sense work overtime.

Partner knows when I'm under the pressure of a dynamic personal stress. He feels it in the harness. He picks up on every nuance and never misses even the most subtle changes in the rhythm of our work. I suppose that my body chemistry is giving off a different smell, and in those moments he struggles to compensate by working even harder to ease my concern.

Vocal intonation is as relevant to integrated human interaction as facial expression. Our manner when we're on the telephone is the most interesting way in which we connect without visual support. I am an expert when it comes to telephone communication because for me it's so honest. Since people are not visually interactive when speaking over the phone, they tend to let down the barriers of normal convention, and their true mood is never hidden from the careful listener. How often have you been aware that the person on the other end of the phone has had a bad day? Pauses, sighs, pitch change, intensity, and total vocal nuance paint a complete picture of the person's mood. The truest lie detector available is not a machine; it's in our ability to interpret an individual's voiceprint. I can tell you it is never wrong.

I've often heard friends say that they can see the tension on a person's face. I grasp the same information except that it comes through enhanced vocal imprinting. No two voices are exactly alike, but if you pay attention to intonation, nuance, and rhythm, the vocal picture carries with it all of the gathering capacity of visual acuity.

The most intimate element in our sensory synergism is touch. It can either confirm love or affection, or shatter relationships through violence or through something much more subtle: the coldness of contact when it becomes mechanical. When intimate touch is only routine, a relationship is on extremely rocky ground. In my growth with Patty, we constantly assess our level of intimacy based on the application of what I think of as the touch quotient. It's not necessary to linger in the passion of a long kiss to truly express our love, but when our lips touch the message is dynamic and perfectly clear. It's like sharing a great bottle of Latour burgundy. All of the grapes, nuance, and distinction—all of the blending of its parts come together—appreciated even in the smallest sip. Every piece of our sensory mosaic will find an appropriate place in the puzzle if we have the inner vision to effectively apply it.

Turn Up Your Senses' Volume

Here is where the sensory dynamic really gets exciting: each of the five senses has an individual volume control that can be turned up or down depending on what information we need. The whole is the sum of all its parts and is greater than any one of them. When all your sensory dynamics come together, they can be relished completely. This is the unrivaled, untapped treasure of sensory synergism. And this common sense approach is available to all of us. You already have this skill. It's just a question of application and taking the time to learn, so let's consider some exercises that you can easily perform in order to expand your sensory synergism.

When our children were very little, Patty and I lived on Cape Cod in the wonderful seaside town of Scituate. Fresh produce was always readily available, and as a new bride, Patty really worked to stretch her wings in the kitchen. She was constantly preparing mouth-watering dishes with fresh vegetables, seafood of all types, and a great supply of freshly grown herbs she planted just outside our kitchen window. I couldn't wait for her experiments, and thank goodness our children were not fussy eaters. When Patty would be making bouillabaisse or clam chowder, shrimp salad or baked stuffed lobster, the children and I would sit in the living room just out of sight of the kitchen and play a special sensory game. I called it "What's Mommy Doing?" With a child on each knee, I'd ask them to describe Patty's activities. They quickly learned that when they heard her using the cutting board, she was probably slicing fresh bread, confirmed by smell as it came out of the oven. They loved to hear the steam rise as the clams or lobsters boiled and anticipated the drawn butter Patty prepared to enhance the taste of the shellfish and fresh corn on the cob.

They also came to know the names of many of the herbs and spices Patty used in her cooking. Oregano was their favorite herb, and Patty used it in the homemade tomato sauce she poured over her hand-rolled pastas. I loved to make the children close their eyes and taste the ingredients individually that went into the meal.

All of these disciplines have served my children well. My son is a carpenter and a musician who appreciates every sensory nuance, from the music he writes to the surfboards and cabinets he builds out of various woods and other materials. My daughter loves to hike the Colorado mountains, and when she describes the natural plant life of the area, she always discusses various types and species in terms of smell or taste and never misses the chance to tell me about a meadowlark or other songbird common to the area.

Work to turn the volume up and down on each of your individual senses, focusing on the specific pieces of sensory information you wish to learn more about. Try eating a meal emphasizing smell rather than taste. Touch a flower rather than smell it. Hear a bird in flight rather than watch it. Change the context of your sensory learning experience, and you'll quickly find that you have become rich in awareness beyond your wildest dreams. With effective application of sensory synergism, I believe your appreciation for life will jump off the Richter scale.

Over breakfast with my running friends, we often talk about the runner's high found in the release of endorphins that categorizes intense cardiovascular activity. Many of you who read this book may not want to go through the effort of becoming a runner, but you have a natural high that's readily available. It's the integration of your common senses through sensory synergism. The great thing about this high is that there is no risk involved, only reward. You don't have to take drugs or swallow gigantic doses of ginseng or ginkgo in order to get it. You just have to open your mind to the sensory possibilities available. Let yourself become passionate about the world around you.

If you live in the city, go out and get excited about the sensory energy. I grew up in Boston and used to love to go with my father to the south end where Italian restaurants prepared all kinds of culinary delights and peddlers with pushcarts sold fresh produce and vegetables on the corner. As a young musician beginning my show business career, I haunted the jazz clubs in cities like New York and New Orleans, spending time in the Village or listening to Dixie in the French Quarter. Then there were the times when the city was quiet during a heavy snowstorm. It was great to walk through normally busy streets and not hear cars while tasting snowflakes on my tongue.

No matter where you live, the senses will expand the value you place on life. Become passionate about the world around you. I bet we can solve some of the environmental problems that we will face in the twenty-first century if we become passionate about our senses. If our passion for sensory synergism is expanded, I believe our social conscience will encourage us to continue to protect our natural resources. Inculcate this concept into the way you educate your children, and allow them to become the generation that may truly appreciate the world in which we live. If we open our minds to these unlimited possibilities, we can exist on a higher plane of what I think of as true sensibilities. In that place, I believe we can better appreciate each other. Communication can be enhanced tenfold, and we can gain a far better understanding of where each of us is coming from.

Seeing Lessons Reflections and Exercises

Are we getting the most out of all of the possibilities? Absolutely not. People are missing the greatest opportunity offered to everyone in the whole of creation. I am excited by my absolute certainty that with effective application you can be as in tune with the senses as anyone on Earth. All you have to do is pay attention to all of the information that's coming to you over the sensory network.

Right now, the information is probably either ignored or jumbled. My guess is you haven't learned to disseminate—that is, separate out—each signal that's coming in. It's a lot like working with your radio dial to clear up a fuzzy station. Maybe you're able to juggle the tuner to get better clarity, or maybe you move the radio around to get its antenna pointed in the right direction, in order to pick up the broadcast. The point is, you make adjustments to improve the quality of the reception. Exercising the senses allows us to learn how we might better isolate each of the senses, then put them together in various combinations, providing us with remarkable collective input.

Let's consider some fun possibilities. If you are sighted, recognize that sight is your dominant sense, just as sound provides me with a larger percentage of my sensory information. So while sitting in your backyard on a spring morning, either close your eyes or go to the extreme by placing a blindfold over your face. Now start to move the individual volume controls of your senses up and down. As I write these pages, I'm sitting on our patio. I can hear cars far off in the distance. I can count thirteen different bird songs. There are some men working on the construction of a new house somewhere down the hill—I love the sound of their saws and hammers as they work to create something beautiful.

Now the wind is rustling the trees, so our wind chimes are active as the breeze creates its own free-form melodic improvisation. I'm working to center my concentration on one individual sound that's a little harder to pull in. It's the bell buoy ringing off San Pedro Point. It tells me what kind of surf my son, Tom, may have if he chooses to go out today. In order to hear it, I'm attenuating its sound forward in my concentration.

To really understand this dynamic of volume adjustment, consider your sense of sight and deal with your capacity to focus your own visual acuity. I'm astounded at what can be done with the eye, from seeing vast expanses of landscape to honing in on the tiniest splinter in the finger of a child. I am amazed when I think about a person's visual capacity and the ability to expand or contract focus as necessary.

That's exactly what I want you to do with each of your other senses. The process will take work; you'll have to practice. Sound will probably develop quicker than smell, touch, and taste. But the game is really fun, and the result will profoundly expand your potential for growth and greater understanding of the world you live in. When I've worked with kids, who are open vessels of possibility, I've seen them expand their sensory dynamic by at least 50 percent. You hold the potential to increase your sensory acuity by at least 50 percent too. I'm not kidding.

Your exercises don't have to be as formal as counting birds or closing your eyes and recognizing the significance of things you touch. You don't need to become a sensory sommelier over a myriad of tastes; you just have to say to yourself, in any given life experience, "I will not take my visual input as the be all and end all of my understanding. I will expose all of my other senses to the circumstances in which I find myself, and with this commitment, my quality of life will take on a remarkable new level of exciting passion."

And how about a fresh understanding of others by applying effective use of the senses? So much can be learned from the nuance of speech. Only a few of us are good enough actors to alter our voice sufficiently to fool a discerning ear. Where people are coming from is obvious if you learn to listen to pitch, rhythm, and inflection. As another sensory exercise, during your next telephone conversation try to draw impressions about the person on the other end. Decide what kind of a day this person is having. Could he or she be having problems at work or at home? And then, as subtly as you can, ask if things are okay.

You'll be surprised at how ready people are to talk about things that are bothering them if they are simply asked. The sound of a smile, the nuance of a sigh, the stuttering over nervous intention, the fear of relationship—all of these things and more are conveyed by the human voice.

Learn to read handshakes or hugs in order to grasp a person's behavioral intent. Assess another's comfort zone by the toxicity of personal smell. And learn to read body language when defining the way in which someone creates his or her own personal space.

The roadmap of sensory dynamics offers all kinds of routes to get to the same goal, allowing us to come to a more complete awareness of where others are coming from. When Thoreau wrote of the state of communion he experienced at Walden Pond, he was not only reflecting on the balance between humans and nature but on the synergism of the senses as they gathered the information confirming that we are vibrantly alive. He understood in every way the link between mind and body, and that the bridge to the collective concept of life is found in the senses.

So build up your senses by cross-collateralizing their effectiveness. Don't just smell a flower—touch it. Don't just watch a bird in flight—listen to it. Don't record snap judgments based on visuals—hear the message from the heart expressed in the nuance of tone and voice. Become intimate and loving through the touch of another while drinking in the smell that makes that person different from anyone else. Become sensitized in the ways in which you gain information that expands your human capacity. Using your senses in new ways will allow you to step beyond compartmentalizing them so that you can enter a wondrous world in which sensory synergism provides you with levels of understanding far beyond your expectations.

Am I high on the senses? You bet. Simply put, they are sensational and available to every one who pays attention to the messages they send and learns to inculcate those messages into a life filled with natural sensory treasures.

Live a Life of Interdependence

Intimate relationships cannot substitute for a life plan.
But to have any meaning or viability at all, a life plan
must include intimate relationships.
—HARRIET LERNER

A Story of Snow and Love

We glide through a world of silence interrupted only by the almost imperceptible sound of snow falling on the branches of the aspens bordering the ski run known as Mary Jane Trail in Winter Park, Colorado. Although I can't hear her, I know my daughter, Blythe, is never more than a foot away, skiing in the tracks I make as we float down the mountain.

It is a perfect Colorado powder day. Champagne, the locals call it, light enough to feel almost transparent as we move through it. In the silence our breathing seems to take on an aspect of gigantic proportion, like a movie with the audio turned up. Breathe out as you sink into the turn. Suck in the much-needed air as you rise, gliding through the powder. Keep your shoulders over the tips of your skis and press your hands down the hill. Turn your skis and follow your knees, they say. But in powder, every motion needs to be exaggerated.

I feel the snow fly over my shoulders and whoop with delight, believing I am virtually weightless in my downhill flight. We come to a narrowing of the trail and Blythe's voice cuts in, "Hold the next turn, Dad. Traverse the hill. Go, go, go, go. And turn, and turn, and turn. Bumps coming. And turn. Slow down. Traverse the hill. And turn. Let 'em run, Dad. Let 'em run." She has just guided me through a transition to the lower part of the hill. And again, she is quiet and I am free.

I hear the sound of the chairlift below and drop into a tuck, bringing my skis together with my butt nearly touching the snow. Thirty, forty, maybe even fifty miles an hour. I feel the wind but do not hear it as the zephyr is absorbed by the soundproofing of the snow. Forty exhilarating seconds later, Blythe's voice cuts in again. "Coming up on your left, Dad."

I switch the poles to my right hand with my left arm extended. In a seamless connection of love and skill, our hands join and we are skiing as one, turning together in an intimate ballet reserved only for those bonded in trust. This is the ultimate in blind skiing. Her hand moves up and down to indicate when I should turn, and I read the degree and intensity of the movement according to the effort she is making. Edge and release, glide and slide. We ease into the chairlift line with the precision of a docking in space.

"What do you think, Blythe?" I ask. "Should we go up again?"

"Are you kidding, Dad? This is the best powder of the season. Or are you getting too old and your legs are fried?"

A challenge from my daughter. "Hey, if you can handle it, no problem. Let's go."

Halfway up the ascent, we're not quite as sure. It's now a full-fledged Colorado dump and I figure they'll close the mountain before we reach the top. Blythe's voice conveys her apprehension, although she expresses it lightly. "It's a whiteout, Dad. I'm as blind as you." We're not fooling around anymore. Both of us understand that and we wonder if it might be better to stay in the lodge at the top of the mountain and have a hot chocolate. But no, we're the Sullivans, undaunted and maybe a little foolish. We grope our way to the take-off point of the trail with conditions still getting worse.

"Hey, Blythe," I ask, a little of the macho worn off. "How bad is it?"

"Dad, I can see the trees on the side of the run, so we won't hit anything. But I can't feel up or down."

I understand exactly what she means.

In a whiteout, all perspective is gone for people with sight and you literally might be moving across the hill just as easily as you might be headed straight down. And yet there is a real excitement in this moment because I know exactly where the vertical is. Skiers talk about a mountain as having a fall line—a slant where gravity and inertia pull you left or right across the hill. My special kinesthetic feel lets me know exactly how to compensate and keep us headed right down the middle.

Forget the trees, I think. Let's just ski. For the first time in our mountain sharing, I will guide my daughter. "Keep your eyes on the trees, kid. I'll do the rest."

Mary Jane Trail has five pitches on the way down separated by flat areas where you can let your skis run. I literally know them all as if I could see them, and on this day, the combination of a daughter's eyes and a father's feel allows us to navigate through the storm in total safety. The loving interdependence makes the experience unforgettable. What a story we'll have to tell in the warmth of the après-ski bar.

What Is Interdependence? My Story

The concept of *interdependence* isn't new. It's an idea that all of us fundamentally understand. Seasons depend on each other to create full Fall harvest. The food chain is part of the natural order, linking us interdependently to all other species. Bringing life into the world arises from a decision made by two people to create a human being.

Just take a look at the world I entered fifty years ago. At that time, people with a disability were thought of as helpless, society's burden, to be pitied and swept under the rug. Of course, there were exceptions like Helen Keller and some of the servicemen injured in World War II. But for the most part, society was in the Dark Ages when considering the possibilities for people with physical limitations or mental challenges to live normal lives.

When I was about 12 weeks and my parents first realized that something was wrong with my eyes, they did what all families do, beginning with a frantic search to try to find the answers. They brought me to the finest ophthalmologist in the world, a German doctor named Veerhoff. This guy did not possess a modicum of bedside manner or human concern. After examining my eyes carefully, he turned to my parents and said without any preamble, "Mr. and Mrs. Sullivan, your son is blind. Institutionalize him." The legend goes that my father tried to punch the guy out. I don't know if that's true, but the pain the doctor inflicted on my parents was unforgivable.

My early life consisted of restrictions and limits. As a blind child beginning to crawl, I learned early to do it backward. It's easier for your feet to hit something than your head. Developing a sense of distance and space is a process of trial and error. My parents put a gate up in front of the stairs because in my toddler stage I fell down the stairs twice. No real damage but pretty scary. I was always holding on to someone's hand or being carried by a loving relative. Thank God, I had a vivid imagination and loved to listen to the radio. In stories of the Old West, I rode with the Lone Ranger as his Tonto. I flew to Mars with Tom Corbett's Space Cadets and solved crimes with the Gangbusters. Through this medium of storytelling I knew there was a world out there that I wanted to be a part of, but how?

When I was nine years old, something interesting was going on next door. Every day I heard the sound of hammers and saws, electric drills, and the voices of men as they built a house right next to mine in the Irish Catholic neighborhood of West Roxbury, Massachusetts. Who would live there, I wondered, and would they have any *kids*? Up to that point, I had gone to a school for the blind and was doing very well. But I had no friends in the outside world.

From Monday to Friday, I was popular. But when I'd come home on weekends, I was limited to the activities my folks provided in the fenced-in backyard where I played games of make believe.

But on the most important day of my life, something was different. I was home from my boarding school on Easter vacation. The neighborhood public schools were on a different schedule and I listened longingly to the sound of the boys and girls as they came and went from the school at the end of the street. And then, wonder of wonders, I heard the door of the new house open and the voice of a child call, "We're home, Mom. Got a snack?" It sounded like a little boy. And then I got a double dose. Another voice, maybe a brother, saying, "It's on the table, Billy. Can't you see it?" This was Mike Hannon, Billy's older brother. I had to figure out how to meet the boys who would rescue me from the prison of my backyard. The fence my parents had put up to keep me safe was chain link, but I had no idea how high it might be. Could I climb it? And if I did, then what? Jump? To a blind child, each step places him at peril. I remember always thinking, will I get hurt? What's the distance from my feet to safe ground when I step off the curb or move from one surface to the other? But I was committed. I had to meet these guys and find a way to connect.

Reaching up, I grabbed the chain link as high as I could and began to climb. The toes of my oxford shoes scrambled for footholds. I could have been Sir Edmund Hillary on Everest for all I knew. Spikes at the top gashed my palms, but I had to go on. Why I didn't believe I could climb down the other side rather than jump is a question I still can't answer to this day. But as my feet reached the top, I launched myself like a baby bird falling from the nest, landing in a heap on the other side, surprisingly unhurt. And there was the little boy's voice again—this time close at hand. "Wow!" he said. "That was a great fall. Are you okay?" I was more than okay. In that moment of perilous rescue, I had gained the ultimate reward: his respect. "Yeah," I said, trying to hide the pain. "I guess it was."

"I'm Billy Hannon. What's your name?" "Tom Sullivan," I told him. "And I'm blind." "Wow!" he said again. "That's wild. Want to play?" Those three words changed my life forever.

Want to play? The most important question I've ever been asked. Yes. Yes. *Yes!*

But how? How would a blind child interact in little boy games in a way that allowed both children to grow and gain the most from the experience? Because no two people are exactly alike and all of us bring individual talents to life, interdependence should occur as the natural order of things. In the case of two boys, it was in the way we designed our play. Billy taught me to throw a baseball with his brother, Michael, acting as our catcher. Mike would bang his fist into his glove and I learned to throw pretty accurately at the sound. Because I wanted to be part of the game, I was willing to spend hours pitching batting practice to the brothers and making it easier for them to make it in Little League. On the other hand, I was part of the wrestling team at the School for the Blind, and Billy and Mike became my sparring partners. Boy, they took a beating but loved the experience. I couldn't really shoot a bow and arrow or a BB gun, but I taught them to appreciate the sound of our wooden swords clanging against the tops of garbage can shields we used as we became King Arthur or Robin Hood and his Merry Men. Billy would describe what was happening as we watched a television show. I taught him how to tell a scary ghost story. We rode a tandem bicycle all over the neighborhood. And when it snowed, we would go double on a sled on the big hill behind the neighborhood school. He's still my good friend to this day.

.   .   .

Although Billy changed my life, he could not alter the general perception that I was blind and that my disability made me a dependent person. In my teens and early twenties, I raged against the system, sometimes rather obnoxiously. My intense desire to be completely independent made me never accept help from people when I was traveling on my own with the use of a cane.

How much easier would it have been for me to take someone's arm and walk across the street rather than step out in the middle of traffic and hear the screech of brakes when I misread the pattern of stoplights? How often did I knock over displays in crowded department stores when I was trying to shop on my own? Sometimes the colors of my clothes didn't match because I wouldn't ask my roommates for help in sorting out my closet.

Then there was my obsession with risk. To be independent, I felt I had to be more daring than anyone else. I was always the kid who climbed higher in a tree, inviting a fall from the thin branches. Or jumped off the garage roof into a snowdrift, hoping it was deep enough and soft enough for a safe landing. Why did I insist on driving a car and endangering my friends? I postured an attitude that made it obvious I could make it on my own. Just watch out world, here I come.

No relationship expressing interdependence is more perfect in its union than the one I share with Partner, my seven-year-old German shepherd guide dog. Not only has our work become efficient, seamless, and beautiful to watch, but the way in which we communicate is almost telepathic.

It's been years since I expressed what could ever be construed as a formal command. Most of the time, I just talk to Partner. For example, when entering a hotel lobby, I may ask him to find the front desk. Since he does not read English, he may take me to the car rental counter or the bell captain, but by simply saying to him, "No, next one, Partner, next one," he'll keep trying until he gets it right. In an airport, I don't have to tell him to find the jetway leading to an airplane—he does it automatically. When attending a conference, he'll pick out an empty chair in a room of thirty, and when we travel alone, I can't help letting him sleep on the other side of the king-sized bed.

He's always willing to work and is completely alert. I provide him with purpose and unconditional love. Our mutual desire to succeed and get it right makes us an unbeatable team.

Domestic Interdependence

I remember early on in our relationship that Patty was upset with me for one reason or another. Too many years have gone by for me to remember why. She expressed her displeasure with *The Look*. All sighted people understand The Look. It's conveyed when you are angry or disappointed with your loved one. I don't really know what it is, but everyone tells me that once you've seen The Look, you'll remember it. Not so in our situation. You could give me The Look from now until hell freezes over and I'd never get it.

So what's left for a frustrated Patty? She had to learn to talk to me, to articulate what was bothering her, to frame her point of view. For a young woman who was from a family of seven brothers and sisters where no one got a word in edgewise, it was easy to be a little shy when expressing what she really thought. For Patty, learning to express herself verbally represented a huge growth in her personality.

We have always read together. In fact, until the dawning of

voice actuation provided me with the ability to read printed materials on my own, one of Patty's principal jobs was to keep me up to date on the affairs of the world or whatever else I was interested in, including sports.

We had just come back from a trip to Florence, Italy. I can never thank Patty enough for creating word pictures of beautiful frescoes, paintings, and Michelangelo's sculptures. She is poetic in her descriptions even though she doesn't believe it.

We have a mutual interest in blind children and their families, and Patty has been active in raising millions of dollars on their behalf. She serves on a number of nonprofit boards in our community and is a leader, demonstrating strength, wisdom, and infallible instinct. These are all qualities that she had long before I met her, but it's clear to me that over the years our intimacy, love, and mutual respect have helped project them forward and her personality has blossomed and grown.

I, too, have changed and grown. I'm no longer compelled to fight life's battles alone. There is this person who believes so fundamentally that I am valuable that I have been forced to become the best Tom Sullivan possible. That's the wonder of the state of interdependence. People rise to a level of ultimate expression when they are buoyed up by the strength of another.

To love someone is to recognize imperfection as God's way of keeping life interesting.

Enlightened interdependence occurs when we gain the maturity to recognize that the search is to find another who brings us to completion as a human being.

I'm no longer afraid of a misstep or a fall when I choose a course for my life's journey because there's always Patty's gentle hand on my arm and her loving heart acting as a sounding board when I'm trying to make a difficult decision. I have no fear of taking on a challenge because I know that her belief in me is total and that she will provide the support system that will allow me to rise to the pinnacle of my own potential.

Interdependence is an effective way to love and is ultimately beneficial for all the parties involved. We now have the Internet superhighway bringing us even closer together in the sharing of information and opportunities for economic and personal growth. We are culturally more homogeneous than at any time in history, and although there are dangers that go with assimilation, the benefits far outweigh the loss of identifiable differences.

In truth, interdependence arises from our recognition of the significance we place on another person. My strengths and talents must be valued by you if we're going to achieve a balance of interdependent equality. It was only when Patty taught me how to appreciate being interdependent that I found the comfort zone necessary to deal with being blind. I now understand that I give as much as I get in every meaningful relationship.

Seeing Lessons Reflections and Exercises

We are all consigned to a life of interdependence. Some of us accept the premise easily, and others rail at the idea that they have any necessary attachments. Unless you're confined to a desert island—and even there, you are dependent on the food chain to survive—you must live in symbiotic interdependent relationships. Here's the bottom line:

Life takes on far greater meaning and is a much more joyous experience

*if you embrace the concept of interdependence with your total being—
heart, mind, body, and soul.*

Place true value on other people, and you will be valued in
turn. Work every day at valuing people—not belittling them,
judging them, or pushing them away because you don't think
they're worthwhile.

With the world changing so rapidly and becoming more and
more impersonal, interdependence commits us to maintaining our
own humanity as we interact to celebrate and preserve our community.

Grow Stronger through Your Turning Points

I love the man that can smile in trouble, that can gather strength from distress and grow brave by reflection.
—THOMAS PAINE

The Miracle of 13

I can still count the seconds, and the order of events is still as clear and detailed as if I were watching it in a film. Even though nearly thirty years have passed, my memory has only sharpened. It was June, and the morning fog had lifted, giving way to a southern California sun that warmed rather than burned. My wife, Patty, had gone to the store to pick up some groceries, leaving me in charge of our two children—three-year-old Blythe and one-year-old Tom. While our little boy napped peacefully, Blythe pulled on my arm, begging in her sweet little girl voice for me to take her swimming. "In a little while," I said, slightly irritated. "Daddy has to work."

At that time my work was hoping that a record company would deem me worthy of putting my music out on vinyl. We had come to California in order for me to chase the dream of becoming a recording artist. With very little money in the bank and the prospects looking dim, I was stressed.

Here we were living in Beverly Hills in a house with a pool we couldn't afford and I sat in the living room praying that the phone would ring while my little girl pulled on my arm. "Come on Daddy, come on Daddy, let's swim," she intoned. "In a little while, Blythe. Just give me a little while. Go play, dear. Find something to do."

The sound of the telephone ringing caused me to react like a horse in the starting gate at the Kentucky Derby. My hands flew for the receiver, then hovered. Don't be too anxious, I reminded myself. Let it ring a couple more times. What if it's just a bill collector, or a friend, or my mother? Why am I so wired? Say a prayer and answer it.

The voice on the other end seemed like a gift from God. "Hello, Mr. Sullivan? I'm the head of the Artist Relations Department at MGM Records. We're very interested in your demo, and we'd like to talk to your representatives about a deal." I started to shake and had to work to keep my voice controlled. All my concentration was focused on this conversation. There was so much at stake.

Had I been able to see, I would have noticed Blythe skipping lightly through the living room. I would have stopped her before she opened the sliding glass door. I would have warned her not to get too close to the edge of the pool. And I would have grabbed her in time to stop her from falling, with a slight splash I did not hear, into the water.

We finished making arrangements. Thank God I hung up the phone and called her name, a little guilty that I had put off our swim. "Blythe?" No answer. "Blythe?"—a little more urgency in my voice—"Blythe?" a parent's instinct beginning to tie my stomach in knots, causing my heart to beat quicker, constricting my throat, my head tingling with panic. *"Blythe?"* The panic was real as I was forced to recognize the possibility. *Move legs, move. Get me outside. Oh my God—the door is open, she must be—oh my God, Blythe!* "BLYTHE!"

The seconds began to tick off. How long had she been in the water—five, ten, fifteen minutes? I wasn't sure. Catapulting into the pool, I thrashed in mad circles, calling, pleading, praying her name. Chlorine and tears stung my face as a blind man played a life-and-death game of bluff. I was crying uncontrollably now, unable to speak or scream, because in the moment I understood beyond doubt that I was truly disabled—a young man without sight who'd done so much that now seemed insignificant.

Music? Career? So what. Harvard educated? What did it matter? Athlete? Who cares? Husband? How could Patty live with me after this? And father—responsible to love and protect? Abject, complete, total failure. Finally out of breath, I stood still, shoulder deep in the water, giving vent to an uncontrollable anger.

I am angry with you, God, angry at the joke that you're perpetrating on a mortal man. I am blind—we both know that—and now you are allowing my blindness to force me to pay the ultimate price—the loss of a child created in innocence and love. Don't do this. Help me. I'm not bargaining, but if you help me, I promise that my life will be a testimony to good works.

Do you believe in miracles? I do. But I also believe in the unfailing capacity of humans to do remarkable things. And looking back over the course of my life since that day in June, I believe that miracles happen when ordinary people do extraordinary things.

I heard it: the blip, blip, blip of her air bubbles as they tracked their way to the surface. Blip, blip, blip . . . I followed them and dove down to the bottom of the pool, my hands extended, clawing at the tiles, groping and hoping to find her. First her foot, leading to her leg, then her torso. My arms wound around Blythe's waist. With all of my strength, I burst to the surface.

What happened next still astounds me. Holding the fifty-pound child in my hands, I found the side of the pool and leaped onto the deck without climbing out. Blythe's head lolled over my shoulder. I listened for her breathing—nothing. I touched her wrist, searching for a pulse that only fluttered. I understood that I had to expel the water from her lungs. Hating myself, I pounded on her small ribs and back. She vomited. Now, down onto the pool deck with my mouth pressed on hers, I breathed into her mouth, then pushed on her chest. Once, twice, three times, four times, five . . . *please let the machine start* . . . six, seven, eight . . . how much time had elapsed? My mind reviewed the seconds. I believed that it had been maybe a minute to a minute and a half since I hung up the phone. Nine, ten, eleven—"Please breathe, Blythe, *please breathe!*"—twelve, thirteen.

Thirteen is not unlucky for me. On the thirteenth blow and push, I heard the soft exhalation of breath that opened my daughter's airway to lungs and life. The gossamer thread of her life was sustained in the softest sound I've ever heard, akin to the cooing of a dove but far more beautiful in its import. Blythe Sullivan, my love, my heart, breathed. And in a few more minutes, she cried, then placed her arms around my neck and said, "Daddy, Daddy," over and over again.

It wasn't until much later that I realized the life-altering effect this event would have on me and our family. It was, however, a major local news story. Cameras literally poked their lenses into our house trying to get a look at our little girl. Interviewers clustered to get the story of a guy they thought was a blind hero. Boy, did they have it wrong. Eventually I wrote an autobiography, *If You Could See What I Hear*, which was turned into a movie.

But now I'm here, twenty-five years later and with twenty-five years of experience to draw on, and an acute awareness that on a June afternoon I became a different and better person. I believe all of us are offered the chance to manifest our best selves when we face turning points, and we're presented with a number of these watersheds in which our choices are made crystal clear.

It's been said that character counts, and these turning points offer us the best test of our capacity to demonstrate character. Whether turning points are based on moments of struggle or triumph, how we put them to the best use is a constant. Nearly losing Blythe on that June afternoon in the family swimming pool definitely prompted me to reconsider what was important in my life. From that moment on, my family came first; my work came second; and hobbies, diversions, and friendships filled up the remaining time and space.

I began to appreciate the positives that came with my disability, and I never again asked, "Why me?" I treasured the relationship I had with my children. Fatherhood became my priority, and in that loving and nurturing process, the best of my own character began to emerge.

What Are Your Turning Points?

Let's consider these turning points in general terms that define what we ought to be looking for. Obviously, we begin with moments of parental impact, and each of us can point to experiences when something our parents did or said affected us greatly. In my case, it was the first time I understood what my parents meant when they talked about me as blind. Right from the beginning, I was told that being blind was only one part of who I was and that I didn't have to be limited by my disability.

Here are some other turning points to think about:

- Relationships with siblings
- The relationship you have with your first friend
- The first day of school
- The first successes in your life—sports, school, the arts
- Your first date
- Falling in love
- Graduating from college
- Getting married
- Your first job
- Career changes
- Becoming a senior citizen
- Coping with illness
- Facing death

All of these events and so many more mark the turning points that shape us, defining our present and framing our future.

The central issue that must be assessed when examining the effect of turning points is whether you see the glass as half empty or half full. When I consider all of the options that life offers to every person inhabiting this planet, I have no patience with those who see the glass as half empty. There are just too many wonderful things to do. And all clouds do have silver linings if we evaluate them as necessary stop signs along life's journey.

It takes courage to launch in a new direction when a turning point is presented, but if we don't choose to try, we will never gain the summit of success. Winners see the glass as half full and see every turning point as an opportunity. And we learn and grow from failure. I have failed greatly—not just once or twice.

A Writer's Life

My friends who make their living as scribes seem to believe that somewhere inside them they have the great American novel just waiting to be put on paper; and I was no exception. Actually, I didn't think I'd write the great American novel; I believed I could be the next Tom Clancy or Robert Ludlum, developing pieces of intrigue, espionage, or psychological thrillers. And that was the direction I chose. I created a character named Brendan McCarthy, a blind psychiatrist who, using highly tuned sensory skills, instinct, and clinical data, would solve serial killings and crimes of passion. The idea sounded great. I figured people would want to read my stuff, and I invested two years writing the first of what I thought would be a series of page-turners.

I even went to the expense of hiring a highly qualified editor to work on my four hundred–page manuscript. His evaluation said, "You are obviously intelligent, and highly gifted. But it is impossible for me to believe that someone with your background, creative instincts and education could write something that is simply a literary disaster. Your plot doesn't hold, you don't get the most out of your characters, and your style, well, there isn't one."

How about that for a shot in the stomach? Two years of work reduced to throwaway pulp. Just to be sure he was right, I also asked my literary agent to read the material. He was even more succinct: "I can't sell it, Tom. That's the way it is." Wham, bam. The blows kept on coming. I had been shattered as a novelist. Two years of painstaking work ending in failure. "Do what you do best," my wife Patty said. "Touch people's lives. Be Tom Sullivan—that's always been good enough."

And that's exactly what I've done. At a painful turning point, I realized that my job was to touch and motivate others with ideas and stories in books like this, and in the movies of hope and triumph I'm privileged to make. What could have been a negative turning point allowed me to focus on the qualities I believe make Tom Sullivan special, rather than on a dream that didn't fit the character I had become. Although turning points can be positive or negative experiences, the question of what we do about them is absolutely fundamental.

Learning curves can flow from turning points.

A positive experience misused does not create a positive result. A turning point that manifests itself as a negative—that is, the death of a loved one, a serious illness, the loss of a marriage—can still provide us with opportunity for growth and even a better quality of life if we approach it as the glass half full, as completely involved and enthusiastic human beings.

A Nation's Turning Point

Turning points also find their way onto history's stage. Americans were shaken to their souls by September 11, 2001. You don't need me to wax on about how the effects of the tragedy touched us all. We just have to look to our memories and our hearts to bring back the shock and pain of a violated nation. But consider how the country has been changed by this historical turning point. Prior to September 11, our national conscience had become convoluted, confused, even abusive. We seemed to have become a nation of rights rather than responsibility, and selfish rather than selfless was the modus operandi under which most of us lived.

All of that changed on September 11. Patriotism pervaded the national consciousness, and the outpouring of contribution and kindness to relief funds was remarkable to witness. We came together as a people and lifted ourselves from our national pain to heights not seen since World War II. Our president seems to have found his voice and is leading forcefully, decisively, and with confidence. Does the person make the moment, or the moment make the person? It's all measured by our willingness to maximize the opportunity presented at our turning points.

Seeing Lessons Reflections and Exercises

In 1981, another president was tested when bullets from an assassin's gun came within centimeters of ending his life. Ronald Reagan rose to the moment, telling his doctors that he forgot to duck, and remarking to a nurse as she took his pulse and held his hand that he hoped Nancy might not find out about the incident. He was more concerned about the wounds to Secret Service agents and his dear friend Jim Brady than he was about himself. And although he was in grave danger, he quickly provided the nation with the confidence to believe that their president would make it and was still strong while he waved to crowds from his hospital room just forty-eight hours after the attempt on his life.

The challenge facing all of us is: Do we get it? Do we know that the experience we're having is a real turning point? Are the antennae out, and are we picking up the important signal that this moment really does count?

Stop and smell the roses. Plug in to these special moments. You generally know when they happen. The difference in the way you function is whether you recognize their importance, then clearly define what you're going to do to amplify their effective role in your life.

That's where the glass half-empty/glass half-full philosophy kicks in. It is so easy to lapse into a negative view of any turning point. Consider these experiences:

- A couple goes through the pain of divorce and eventually both people find someone else to love. Hopefully, they bring a more caring approach to their second marriages instead of falling back into conditioning traps that arose from past mistakes.

- You lose a loved one. Beyond your grief, engage in communication with others instead of withdrawing. Continue to have a busy life and value people more because of the loss of someone you cared about.

- You grow older and retire. Don't sit around waiting to die; instead, become active, a Gray Panther, recognizing that for the first time in your life you have the time to do the things you might have always hoped you would be able to enjoy.

- You change careers and move to another town, or you are transferred by your company away from family and friends. See the experience as new doors opening instead of blaming your boss and shutting down from the opportunity to meet new people and involve yourself in your new community.

I see every turning point as a gateway to opportunity. Without turning points, how can we grow? Without turning points, how can we reshape or reinvent ourselves in order to be better than we were before?

Be a person of character. Without difficult decisions and painful moments, you can never appreciate the highs that come from love and achievement. Turning points provide you with a chance to be your best self and rise to levels beyond your expectations. Turning points provide you with the tests necessary to define whether you can live as a person of character.

Turn Your Disadvantages into Advantages through Self-Worth

Adversity has the effect of eliciting talents, which in prosperous circumstances would have lain dormant.
—HORACE

Wrestling for Self-Worth

I was in the seventh grade in 1959 at Perkins School for the Blind in Watertown, Massachusetts. To its credit, Perkins was always trying to find ways to integrate blind kids with their sighted peers. I remember that we used to joke that the sighted children were the "normies," meaning normal. I'm not sure what that made us, but I guess it was sort of a gang mentality, like it was cool to be a member of the normies or the blindies.

One of the things that Perkins chose to do to help us integrate was to get blind guys involved in sports; in the case of track and field, some of the events were modified. For example, the broad jump was a standing broad jump rather than a running one. Thank goodness. I can picture myself flying down a runway as fast as I could hoping that I would hit the board for my takeoff at just the right angle so that I wouldn't jump and break my leg. The same thing was true for the high jump. We lined up to the bar and were only allowed one step before trying to clear the height. When I tried to high jump, I was so bad that after literally breaking the bar by landing on top of it, the coach suggested that I try to find some other event if I was going to participate against the normies.

I discovered wrestling, even though my beginnings could not be thought of as auspicious. Wrestling is a contact sport. The idea is that you grab the other person and throw him on the ground and try to pin him. In this sport, the only modification made to accommodate a blind athlete was to keep the wrestlers in contact when we were in the stand-up position.

I weighed 95 pounds in seventh grade and hoped desperately

that I could succeed at something. The truth was, I was horrible. I lost my first eleven matches in two minutes and twenty-three seconds, never even getting my uniform dirty.

I can still remember in my nightmares the sound of a referee's hand slapping the mat to indicate that I was pinned. Before the twelfth match, the coach told me that the guy I was going to compete against was a much better athlete than I was, so I ought to just go out and do the best job I could, and as he put it, "Try not to be dead." Real positive coaching, right?

For three days before each confrontation with destiny, I believed that I was going to be killed. Even though my mind told me that the kid I was going to compete against was my size, in my head—I suppose because I was blind—my opponent was a monster. I even had nightmares in which he possessed many octopus-like arms, and with these extended tentacles he would squeeze the life blood out of my little body. My panic led to bouts of uncontrollable diarrhea. I became so distraught that on two occasions I walked out onto the mat wearing my uniform inside out.

Both sighted and blind athletes feel the same way before a wrestling match. I guess it goes with the sport. The expectation of failure overwhelms the possibility of success. I bet that everyone reading this book has experienced moments just like that. Those moments may have not been on the wrestling mat, but whether they were in sports, the arts, relationships, or careers, I believe all of you have experienced this feeling of expected failure.

I think there are two kinds of nervousness that we all must deal with: constructive and destructive. I once asked Ervin "Magic" Johnson, the great player for the Los Angeles Lakers, if he got nervous before a playoff game. "I wouldn't call it nerves, Tom," he said, "but I get excited." I believe that's because Magic has always been secure in his skill and talent. So that kind of feeling is constructive nervousness. Destructive nerves come when you not only are anticipating the game but doubt your competence to play it.

Mine was a case of destructive nervousness. Most young wrestlers suffer from destructive anxiety. Just before a match, there are a lot of guys who try to psych you out. They mumble at you while the referee is giving you his instructions, telling you about all the things they're going to do to you. They give you a crushing handshake, suggesting they're stronger than you. When you put your hand on their shoulder before the whistle blows to create contact, they flex their biceps. It's all posturing, but if you're suffering from destructive nervousness, it can scare you to death.

I had a queasy stomach and no confidence going into my twelfth wrestling match. The opponent's name was David Weathersby, and as he crushed my hand in his thirteen-year-old vise-like grip and told me he was going to kill me, something amazing happened to my psyche. I came to the conclusion that if I was going to die, it couldn't get any worse, so I might as well just accept the inevitable, wrestle the match as hard as I could, and let the chips (or the body parts) fall where they may. I literally could feel the tension exorcise itself from my body.

Once I had evaluated the worst possible result, I was able to accept it and begin to consider a positive alternative. Maybe something good could come out of this after all, and it did. I won the match, then went on to have a career in which I was good enough to be elected to the National Wrestling Hall of Fame in Stillwater, Oklahoma.

As I grew in confidence, the concept of turning disadvantage into advantage became fundamental to my success. When going out on the mat to meet my opponent, I would shuffle, seem tentative, and walk with my hands out in front of me like the caricature of a helpless blind man. My handshake would be wimpy, and I would actually make my body quiver in fear. When the referee would blow his whistle, I would even let down my guard to allow my opponent a free shot at my legs. What he didn't know was that inside I was poised for the pancake move. That's when you thrust your body away, landing your chest aggressively on his back while you nearly pull his arms out of their sockets, driving his head into the mat.

So I went on to win a lot of matches. I competed against a guy who was ahead of me eleven to three. One of the complications of my blindness was I suffered from acute glaucoma and had to have my eyes enucleated (removed). The plastic ones are light blue in color, and I'm told, rather attractive. In this particular match, the next time the boy knocked me down, I simply popped out one of the plastic orbs, dropping it on the mat and saying, "Stop. *Stop.*"

My opponent looked down and saw the eye lying on the mat. I could picture what went through his mind and I can certainly remember what he sounded like when he threw up. Somewhere in my old school records it says, "Sullivan, winner by default." And *that* is turning disadvantage into advantage!

Affirm Your Spirit

The application of turning disadvantage into advantage is a most positive affirmation of the human spirit. People who are able to apply this concept as a core belief are way ahead of the game. I've known some gloom and doomers who frame their entire life process around the expectation of failure in order to protect themselves against major disappointments, but *most of these people never become winners because they lack enough personal conviction to fulfill their own potential and become all that they can be.*

I think it's fair to say that being blind has required me to work harder in order to achieve success. I have had to work more diligently and with more attention to detail. In order for me to carry out even the simplest of tasks, I've had to be a meticulous planner and remain disciplined in my effort level and judicious use of time. This was never more evident than during my days at Providence College and Harvard. In order for me to complete the work and pull down decent grades, along with maintaining an active social life and participating in sports, I needed to be completely organized.

Here was a typical day for me at Harvard: I would get out of bed at around 5:30 in order to get to wrestling practice or rowing by 6:00. Morning workouts would end around 7:45 with just enough time to eat a doughnut and get to class. If my classes ended by 1:00, that would allow me three hours to study before returning for afternoon practice. Then there was dinner, usually a sandwich grabbed at Elsie's Roast Beef in Harvard Square, and I would be off to my night job.

Since my parents had separated by this time, I had become my mom's principal support. As a way to make ends meet, I usually wound up those days by playing piano in some nightclub until 1:00 in the morning. Then I would drag my butt home, try to sleep for a few hours, and get up and start all over again.

My hectic schedule was made even more complicated because of the effort necessary to function as a blind person in busy metropolitan Boston. I nearly suffered a nervous breakdown. My life reached a crescendo of complications that was totally overwhelming.

At that time, Harvard Square in Cambridge was being completely torn up with new construction. I often tripped into open manholes in the street, or felt my cane drop into open sewer grates. I couldn't memorize the bus schedule that was forever changing. Cabs were unavailable to bring me home on weekends, as all the streets were closed to traffic.

Having not made many friends, there was no one to help me. And then there was the snow—a blind person's fog, absorbing all sounds and covering the landscape, increasing not only my apprehension and desperation but also the real danger of being hurt. The tension was impossible to bear, but life lessons grew out of that experience that will always allow me to cope with stress:

- Never underestimate the power of a human being to turn even the most difficult adversities into victories.

- When we think of ourselves as less than, or inferior to, our colleagues, friends, families, and others, we cripple our capacity to maintain a positive philosophy.

Negative self-worth can be overcome if we are able to find one gift—just one gift—that we can apply in a positive way to how we see ourselves. We have all known people who are fueled by negative self-worth. The short man who becomes a highly successful athlete or corporate CEO; the overweight woman who ends up having a beautiful body because she hates the way she looks; the shy child who finds that he possesses intellectual or artistic gifts; the minority person who drives her competitive spirit by adopting a stance that overcomes racial profiling.

We can draw on negatives or positives to turn disadvantage into advantage. It's about knowing where you're coming from and committing to an ongoing course of action. I have to admit that I've often been driven by the negative vibes I receive from people. Professionally, when someone suggests that I can't do something because I am blind, I'm inspired to finds ways of proving that person wrong. If I'm confronted with something that seems completely unrealistic and out of my reach, I'm challenged to find a solution; and if I ask a question and get an unequivocal no as the answer, I become almost fanatic in my desire to turn the no to yes.

Following the writing of my autobiography *If You Could See What I Hear,* in 1975 and 1976, I wrote a children's version called *Adventures in Darkness.* I loved that little book. It highlighted the stories of my childhood escapades in the sleepy New England summer town of Scituate, Massachusetts. Over the years, I received thousands of letters from children who had been moved by my adventures.

As with most books, however, the shelf life of *Adventures in Darkness* came to an end, and eventually it went out of print. Three years ago, I received a letter from a boy in Des Moines, Iowa, telling me how much *Adventures in Darkness* had meant to him. He had taken it from the library to write a school book report. I was so moved by what he had to say that I found myself wondering if I could turn this children's work into a screenplay.

"Forget it," my agent said. "It's too soft. Don't waste the time," my producer and director friends told me. "Nobody will buy it." "Tom, you have so much to do," Patty said, "I don't think this is a priority."

With belief and persistence, you can turn all disadvantages into advantages.

I wrote seven drafts of the movie with my writing partner, Alan Katz. Everybody I knew in the business turned us down, until we found Crusader Entertainment, a company committed to the development of films with family values.

Being willing to commit and then staying with the dream is fundamental in maintaining a life built around the idea of turning disadvantage into advantage.

An Inspiring Story

No one I've ever known better exemplifies this philosophy more than my friend Mike Rantz. I met Mike the first Christmas that our family spent in Winter Park, skiing our beloved Rocky Mountains. Mike suffers from severe muscular dystrophy—so severe that when we met he was being carried by members of his family into the offices of the National Sports Center for the Disabled.

Hal O'Leary, the founder of this special program, explained to me that this guy would never ski. "Maybe we could put him in a mono ski. That's the ski that sits on the snow where the speed is controlled by a person tethering. I think that's possible, but he'll never be out there on his own power, standing upright and gliding down the hill on two skis."

Boy, were we wrong. Through hard work, Mike Rantz has not only learned to ski without the aid of any adaptive equipment but has become a major instructor in our program with over twenty years of service to the students who come to this mountain full of miracles. He also has an incredible wife, Jenny, whom he met in our program, and two beautiful girls who are both ranked world-class junior skiers, with hopes to go to the Olympics in 2006 or 2010. Mike's philosophy: "Bubba, anything can be achieved if you work, have patience, take risks, and turn disadvantage into advantage." My pal is proving it every day.

In love won and love lost, experience is our greatest teacher and disadvantage can be turned into advantage. In moments of pain and doubt, we can summon our courage and grow to be better than we ever thought possible. The challenge of our circumstance provides us with the opportunity to be ultimately creative in overcoming adversity, and each of us holds the potential to reach for a higher calling and grow to be our better selves.

Do we always achieve our goals? Certainly not. Do we face disappointment and hurt that weigh us down? Of course we do. Do we sometimes not measure up to our own sense of self-worth? Without question. But committing ourselves to the idea that turning all disadvantages into advantages puts us in the right frame of mind to achieve our goals and become what we believe ourselves to be.

Turning disadvantage to advantage is as simple as deciding to try. It can quickly become a habit that serves you well in a future bright with hope and promise.

Leadership

It was Vince Lombardi, the great Green Bay Packers coach, who first coined the expression, "When the going gets tough, the tough get going." But it was British Prime Minister Benjamin Disraeli who pointed out that great leaders always arise out of chaos. That's because they have the clearest understanding of the principle of turning disadvantage into advantage. They immediately grasp the idea that when times are at their worst and people are most confused, opportunity to mold opinion and to influence others is at its most obvious crossroads.

Remember that people are vulnerable when they are confused, and those human beings who act decisively under stress, even if their course of action is later found wanting, emerge as leaders. Corporate CEOs are not necessarily remembered for the stewardship of stable companies; they become legendary when they turn the company around. Contemporary business is replete with stories of men and women who came to the fore in times of adversity and molded opinion by pointing out the capacity of individuals and groups to turn their disadvantages into advantages.

It usually comes down to getting back to basics. I remember when Lou Gershner took over the chairmanship of IBM. While interviewing him, I asked what he thought it would take to place Big Blue back on the top of the tech world. He snapped, "Doing what we do best, Tom—just doing what we do best." What he really meant was: Always keep it simple. Hone in on those products and values that return us to where we were.

Michael Jordan, the greatest basketball player in the history of the sport, was rejected by his high school basketball coach and didn't even make the squad until he was a junior. By that time, his anger had been fueled, and the disadvantage of sitting on the bench was transformed by his efforts into taking advantage of every opponent throughout high school, college, and the pros. Jordan had an uncanny capacity to rise to the highest level against the greatest odds, and to always want the ball at the last few seconds of crunch times in the biggest games.

Turning disadvantage into advantage builds confidence. I know that all of us take great satisfaction when we do something that others expect us not to be able to achieve. President Jimmy Carter came out of nowhere to defeat the incumbent, Gerald Ford, in 1976. He said, "I was told by everyone that I couldn't win—but I knew that the climate in the country was right for someone to step forward and assert democratic values. The nation wanted the moral higher ground, and I believed I could give it to the people."

Seeing Lessons Reflections and Exercises

Much of turning disadvantage into advantage is being at the right place at the right time. But more of its success comes from knowing that you're at the right place at the right time. It's easy to miss the signs—either because you're insecure and aren't looking, or because you are a negative person, unwilling to look at your capacity to turn any disadvantage into an advantage.

Seeing disadvantage and capitalizing on it—turning it into

advantage—is the central theme on which winners build success. Start by acknowledging your disadvantages and recognizing that turning them around will take hard work. Understand fundamentally that if you can succeed at changing the paradigm of disadvantage, coupled with all of the other things you do well, you will become a winner.

Create a strategic plan in order to get to your goals, and understand that it's necessary to find people of like minds to achieve the intended results. Keep your eyes on the ball and avoid distraction. It is critically important to be single-minded in these most difficult pursuits.

If you can turn your most substantial negatives into positives, the rest of the pieces necessary to provide you with personal success will simply fall into place. Try it and see what happens!

Live with Pride

There is this paradox in pride—it makes some men ridiculous, but prevents others from becoming so.
—C. C. COLTON

Singing Out

In 1976 I was 29 years old. Patty and I were living in southern California, and I was well on the way to a successful career in show business. Our daughter, Blythe, was six, and our son, Tom, was four. We were living the American dream of hard work, creating wealth and prosperity. The Cold War was heating up, inflation was running rampant, and the energy crisis, along with dependence on foreign oil, had us all worried. But most important to Americans was that 1976 was the bicentennial birthday of the nation.

Celebrations were planned around the country, and founding cities, such as Boston and Philadelphia, were getting face-lifts in preparation for the festivities. During Christmas week 1975, I had gotten a phone call from Blanton Belk, my friend and founding director of the international organization Up With People. Blanton had been invited to bring the cast of Up With People to participate in the halftime performance of Super Bowl X, to be held on January 21 at Miami, Florida's famed Orange Bowl.

I could hear the excitement in his voice as he talked about the show that they were planning for over 90 million people tuned in around the world. He asked me if I might be able to help. I thought he meant that maybe I would write some special material for the show. Was I ever surprised when he suggested that I perform the national anthem prior to the game.

Once the surprise had worn off, the significance of what I was going to do set in. It was the two hundredth birthday of the United States. If I could create the spirit of America in my performance, I could strike a small spark that might remind my fellow Americans that we were a blessed people living in a blessed land.

In 1976, the two best teams in pro football were the Dallas Cowboys, coached by Tom Landry and quarterbacked by Navy graduate Roger Staubach, and the Pittsburgh Steelers, coached by Chuck Nole and quarterbacked by strong-armed Terry Bradshaw. Both teams also possessed phenomenal defensive units, with the Steelers nicknamed The Steel Curtain.

The game promised to be a titanic struggle, and that's how it turned out. But as I stood on the sidelines, ready to walk out to the center of the field and perform, my stomach was in knots, and my condition wasn't helped as the public address announcer began: "Ladies and gentlemen," I heard him say, "to honor America with the singing of our national anthem, the cast of Up With People and recording artist Tom Sullivan."

Hearing my name was scary enough, but at the exact moment the PA announcer was introducing us, Pete Roselle, the former commissioner of the National Football League, walked up behind me and placed a big hand on my shoulder. "Young man," he said, "you're going to be performing for 90 million people. It's the bicentennial. Be proud to be an American. When you sing that old national anthem, you're representing the whole nation. So sing it with pride. And good luck!"

I took a deep breath and walked to the center of the field. Twenty-five years later, I am still amazed when I remember the feeling of calm that settled over me as I touched the cold metal of the microphone. "Be proud," he had said. "Sing our anthem with pride."

The notes exploded and soared from inside me as I sang that day. Never before or since have I been so at one with the music, and never did I feel so proud to be an American.

What Pride Means

Fast forward to 1988, when my love affair with football was still going on. Because of a relationship with coach Mike Shanahan of the Denver Broncos, I had been invited to address the team before they played the Cleveland Browns in a championship game that would decide which of these teams would go to the Super Bowl that year. I loved the movie *Dead Poets Society,* starring Robin Williams, so I chose the phrase *carpe diem* (seize the day) as my theme for my presentation to the players.

My friend John Woodward and I had hats made with the insignia *carpe diem* stenciled on the front, and they were a big hit with the guys. But what stood out about that experience was not my speech—it was meeting a friend of head coach Dan Reeves named Cleave McLeary.

McLeary had lost an arm and a leg while serving the Marine Corps during the Vietnam War. He had sacrificed to save his squad in a firefight and been rewarded with the Medal of Honor. Rather than being embittered, McLeary lives his life as a testimony to the power of the human spirit. He has gone on to run marathons, write books, raise a beautiful family, and become one of America's most sought-after motivational speakers.

His philosophy centers around an acronym that he has developed, and I have wholeheartedly adopted, for the word *pride.* Cleave defines it as Personal Responsibility for Individual Daily Effort, and I don't think it's possible to better express a definition and an application of the term. If we examine each part of the definition, I think we easily discover how right on my friend's idea truly is.

1. Be Personal

Pride must be personal. When studying corporations that fail, I've found that the first sign of collapse is when a company's results are no longer personal to every employee.

There can be many reasons why this situation might occur. Either people believe that management isn't committed to their employees, or through an acquisition corporate culture is devastated. And then there are the cases where there has been a change in leadership style, usually from a founder's hands-on participation to a more distant, hands-off approach.

Whatever the cause, the result is predictable. Under stress, people will stop trying, and the blame game will begin. This is certainly what's happening in the role parents play in the education of their children. Whether considering a private school in an affluent neighborhood or a minority school in America's worst ghetto, the success or failure of a student depends on the participation of the parent. All of us have heard people blame teachers or the system for Johnny's bad grades. Forget it. Johnny failed because his parents didn't invest the time to develop their child's success.

I came to understand the personal requirement for educational participation by parents when writing a book called *Special Parent, Special Child* that profiled the lives of parents with special-needs children. In researching the book, I spoke to more than three hundred families, searching for the people and the stories that could best express the common grounds shared by all of the parents.

In every case, the recurring theme was that the parents of a special-needs child could not allow the education of their child to become anything but personal. One parent told me, "It's a war out there, Tom, and I'm a soldier on the front lines." From another I heard, "When I go in for meetings to discuss the individual education plan for my son, I make sure that I'm better prepared than anyone else in the room." A third said, "You have to realize that *nobody* will love your child the way you do, and nobody will understand their specific needs as completely as a parent."

We suffer from a bad habit in our society of placing blame on the collective: *them.* We've all done it. What are *they* going to do about the roads? Are *they* ever going to get our taxes under control? How are *they* going to cope with the rise in violent crime? Will *they* ever get a handle on the environment? We love to blame the collective for our own unwillingness to make issues personal.

2. Take Responsibility

Harry Truman was right when he said, "The buck stops here." There's no avoiding the fact that we are responsible for the decisions we make, whether they are personal or professional, practical or frivolous, moral or immoral. Pride in self and the individual character that makes us who we are can only be achieved when we step forward and take responsibility for our actions.

We all fall off the wagon occasionally when reaching for the moral higher ground, and none of us walks the straight and narrow path to perfection all the time. But personal responsibility needs to be a constant in our lives if we are ever to maintain a committed sense of self-worth.

Granted, there are circumstances that all of us face that seem to affect us beyond our capacity to control. A good example might be how we are affected by a national disaster. But in those moments of national and personal tragedy, do we become people courageous under fire, as in the case of my friend Cleave McLeary, because he felt responsible for his fellow Marines? Or, do we simply stay on the sidelines, uninterested and uninvolved?

Each of us has the capacity to step forward and demonstrate a responsibility that will effect a more positive result—if we simply make the *right* choice. Responsibility encompasses not only our own choices but the way in which those choices affect others, and I believe here we come to a very subtle truth about ourselves.

There are two kinds of people in the world: the selfish and the selfless. In the case of selfish people, I find them to only see the world based on how it affects them, not how they affect it. They carry no responsibility toward others and seem to have no concern for the effect they have on others.

There are also wonderful souls who are selfless and evaluate their decisions based on how they will affect others. They are responsible, and we love and treasure them for their goodness.

3. Invest Individual Daily Effort

Nothing comes easy in life. The trials and tests that mold character seem to be never-ending. People full of pride are willing to invest individual daily effort in the struggle for personal success. No life test better demonstrates this concept than running the 26 miles and 385 yards of a marathon. And it's true that the last 385 yards can be tougher than the first 26 miles.

Life Is a Marathon

I have participated in a number of these endurance efforts, and there's a phenomenon common among all of us who pass the marathon test. The race is never as tough as the individual daily effort required during the training. There are a lot of different approaches that runners adopt when preparing for a marathon, but there's one common element: at least once a week, you're going to get up at some ungodly hour of the morning, usually before the sun rises, put your sneakers on, and take to the road for the long run.

If you're lucky, you'll be out there with some other crazy people who are also getting ready for the event. But more often than not, you will be taking to the road, or the trail, or the bike path by yourself. And as the miles go by and the temperature gets higher, you will at some point in a twenty-mile training run ask yourself, "Why? Why am I out here, thirsty and sore and tired, attempting to do something that in the scheme of things is only important to me?"

You do it because you believe in the individual daily effort necessary to feel proud of yourself when they place that finisher's medal around your neck. Nothing I've ever experienced can duplicate that sense of excellence and pride.

In 1983, I had decided to run the New York Marathon along with my friend Dr. Norman Panitch. There are a lot of marathons in this country, Boston being the most famous, but I don't think any of them can compare to the New York experience. It goes through all of the boroughs, ending in Central Park. When you come off the 59th Street Bridge, the roar from the spectators rises up to meet you as you crest and make your way down the other side, entering Manhattan. No race is as diverse in ethnicity and culture as the New York Marathon; no race is as full of neighborhood smells and textures, and in the encouragement you get from the millions of people who line the course. But in 1983, the temperature soared into the 90s as we took the start line, with the dew point placing the humidity at the saturation level. It was damn hot.

Dr. Panitch and I had decided that this would be the race in which we would break the 3-hour and 30-minute barrier, which translates to running about a mile every 8 minutes—a rather daunting goal for a middle-aged athlete. But as we came over the top of the Triborough Bridge at about 15 miles, we were right on schedule—the time said just under 2 hours.

We were ecstatic. I remember squeezing my friend's arm and

saying, "We've got it made, pal. We just have to keep putting one foot in front of the other, and we've got it."

Have you heard the phrase "hit the wall"? The doc told me that it means all at once you get to a point where your body has run out of glycogen, or sugar stores, to keep going. It begins to literally shut down before something horrible happens to you. I had heard about the wall from runners throughout my racing life, but it had never happened to me—not until that day in the New York Marathon. At 19 miles, within the span of about 50 yards, I hit the wall and literally came to a stop. I wanted to collapse, to simply lie down on the pavement and die.

My mind was telling me to keep going, but every fiber of my body was saying, "No, not today. You're all done, Sullivan. Take your running shoes, look for a cab, and go home." But there was another thought that found its way into my confused brain. I had an obligation to my friend, Norman Panitch. For months we had trained together, in rain and cold, in heat and on hills. We had committed to share this experience as best friends, a modern-day Damian and Pitheus. I could not let my friend down, and I carried a personal responsibility for my own individual daily effort.

The question in my muddled mind was, Did I have the pride and the courage to complete the last 7 miles? There were times during the next 3 hours when I nearly crawled up the hills in Central Park. That's right. We didn't run 3:30 that afternoon. Our time was more like 5 hours. But we each have a medal in our trophy case, and we know how much we shared in love and friendship as we committed ourselves to the agony and the personal responsibility for the individual daily effort necessary to complete the marathon.

Life is a marathon, and we are required to commit ourselves to the individual daily effort necessary to finish the race. There are no short-term solutions. The problems that beset the world, no matter how daunting, can be coped with if each of us makes a personal decision to take responsibility for our own daily effort. Pride is the foundation of our character, both as individuals and as a national theme. We've seen our nation come together at moments of global conflict or natural disaster. We seem to save our best for those times when our best is required.

I believe that each of us possesses the pride necessary to achieve any goal.

Someone once wrote, "If it can be conceived, it can be achieved," and the constant necessity to get to the top of the mountain is the commitment we make to our own personal responsibility for individual effort—pride.

Seeing Lessons Reflections and Exercises

You can't be proud of your own achievements or of your own character if you don't carry a positive sense of self-worth into all aspects of the life process.

How I feel about me will largely determine how I feel about you. There's sort of a mirror between us. As I see your reflection through the glass of evaluation, I compare it to my own sense of personal achievement. If my self-worth isn't in balance, I will feel inferior to you, so I will be unable to live my life as a pride-full person, confidently believing in my ability to add contributions to your life and the lives of others.

Cultivate and nurture the kind of positive self-image that lets you say to yourself, "I'm valuable to you. We can benefit from each other if we are open to recognize the significance we place on each other." False pride occurs when you believe that you are an island—when you think that you don't need me to get you where you hope to go.

This self-pride archetype is the single most dangerous element affecting the way leaders conduct themselves in the relationship they maintain with their followers. When *I* becomes more important than *we*, pride is not in the right proportion. I believe it is completely appropriate to be proud of your own achievements, but resting on your laurels without challenging yourself to climb the next mountain is the quickest way to personal and professional failure.

People who have the pride quotient working correctly let actions speak louder than words. Those who are bombastic and boastful usually have an ego that is completely out of whack and must define their success by telling you about it over and over again. The people I admire most in the world are those who, to quote Theodore Roosevelt, "walk quietly and carry a big stick." They just simply get it done. They operate on a plane of excellence driven by their own personal responsibility for individual daily effort to get it right.

Pride makes you go the extra mile. Put in overtime. Never quit. Never give up. Pride is our saving grace when times get tough, and it is the feeling of celebration you experience when a challenge has been met.

Love People

Some people weave burlap into the fabric of our lives, and some weave gold thread. Both contribute to make the whole picture beautiful and unique.

—ANON

Miracle Workers

Patty and I were being driven to Harpo Productions in Chicago because I was scheduled to appear as a guest on *Oprah*. Of course, Oprah Winfrey is one of America's most prominent and influential women. After appearing on hundreds of television shows over the past twenty-five years, I was surprised that I felt nervous to be meeting this remarkable person.

There are people who cast a big shadow and require us to measure up to the principles and values with which they live their lives. That's how I felt meeting Oprah. By the end of our television experience, I think it's safe to say that both Oprah and I were in awe of the human being who shared the show with us.

A couple of months before, Oprah had received a letter from a twelve-year-old boy named Matty Stepanek. Matty suffers from life-threatening muscular dystrophy. In the course of his young life, he has faced death a number of times.

The show had decided that I would be the second guest, so I sat in the front row of the audience, maybe 12 to 15 feet from the set where Oprah and Matty would conduct the interview. During their time on camera, I wonder if I even breathed—I know I didn't move—because Matty's story was so remarkable, emotional, and inspirational. I understand that my life was forever changed by the spirit of this most remarkable twelve-year-old soul.

Matty is the fourth child in the Stepanek family, but he will no longer spend holidays with his brothers and sisters. They, too, were afflicted with muscular dystrophy and are no longer with us.

Matty's mother, Jenny, has always been a highly motivated

person, a committed parent, a gifted professional, and a terrific athlete who loved even the torture of running marathons. Jenny could never have foreseen that she would contract an adult form of muscular dystrophy after having four children.

How could God bring such havoc and loss to one single family? But it happened, and they were forced to make one of life's fundamental decisions: Do we allow our circumstances to press us down, or do we rise up and find the positives implicit in the basic human desire to survive? So here they were, a mother and son, both wheelchair-bound, trying to figure out how to cope with life-and-death issues that would shatter most of us.

The first thing I noticed was the sound of Matty's portable breathing device punctuating his vocal intonation as he told his story. Of course, the breathing device was supporting the inhalation and exhalation of breath required to keep him alive. But by the end of the interview, I was sure that Matty's spiritual strength—the power of his aura—will survive even if his body does not.

Matty, who describes himself as a peacemaker, had identified three wishes he considered important to fulfill: He wanted to see his poetry published. Both *Heart Songs* and *Journey through Heart Songs* have been on the *New York Times* bestseller list. Matty told us that he also wanted to have the chance to meet President Jimmy Carter (who he eventually did), as he considered the former president and Nobel Prize winner to be the most important peacemaker of our time. And this morning, his third wish was being realized, as he was talking with one of America's most influential women.

One of Matty's poems provides illuminating insight into how he sees himself. I should also note that Matty did the illustrations found in both of his works. In the poem "A Hand Full of Matty, a Self-Described Portrait," the illustration is a tracing of his own hand. The words become self-explanatory:

My fingers stand for reader, writer, Black Belt, collector and
friend.
My palm stands for heart songs, ebullient, spiritual, honest,
trustworthy, brother, uniparental, optimistic, inspiring, diligent, savant, peacemaker and gift of God.
My hands rise in prayer for giving thanks for my being, which
stands for life.

"My being, which stands for life." A life that's been excruciat-
ingly difficult yet joyously positive. A process of ongoing pain but
of the triumph found in the expression of a mind unfettered by illness and limitation; a heart that sings the songs of a spirit; a soul
soaring and pouring out literature and love that will enrich the lives
of all of us fortunate enough to know him or read his works.

Matty tells me that he has met the angels on nights when death
was present in his room. My thinking is that these guardians are
getting to know him because they believe he will be one of them
someday.

Throughout my own life, people have often written wonderful
things about how I have affected them. Their words have always
been flattering and appreciated, but I never took them very seriously. I have always been too busy relishing the life experience to
think about how Tom Sullivan might be affecting others.

Following the show, I asked Matty if he considered the effect his
life and his work were having on everyone he met. "Oh no," he
said. "I'm just doing what I'm meant to do with the time I have."

Giving on a Fast Track

Do you think it's possible that God speeds up the completion of a
life mission when our time on earth may be limited? I've often met

children struggling with terminal illness who seem to be on a fast track to purpose. They accelerate the process of having to get it all done before they cross over and leave us. They carry with them an urgency, understanding the tenuous nature of their lives. We say, "How could they be so wise?" We wonder if they experience any joy.

Matty is joyous. We talked about all the video games he loves and how much he enjoys the company of his peers. During my time on the show, I had discussed the importance of having children to play with. Matty told me it had been very difficult for him to have friends, since he now was forced to have home schooling due to his fragile condition.

Following the show, I found out that when Matty and his mother returned home to Pittsburgh, a wonderful thing happened. There was a knock on the door, and Jenny asked Matty if he would answer it. Two children Matty's age were standing on the front stoop, and my friend had the same experience I had when one of the children asked, "Want to play, Matty?"

I feel Matty and I are kindred spirits. Both of us want to be valuable in life, even though Matty's breaking the speed record, warping out important work, while I'm sort of poking along. Matty is my new hero, and I hope I helped him focus on his self-worth, aiding him in understanding the important role he's playing in the world. That's why the exchange of people is so important: The process is reciprocal.

If you give it, you get it back.

I know there are cynics who think that the world is principally divided into givers and takers, and that we all must protect ourselves against the users—those who only relate to us for their personal gain. I reject that idea. I have never met a human being who did not offer me something, even if I had to work hard to glean something positive from our interaction. In nine out of ten cases, it's easy to find goodness if you look for it. It's not buried under a rock; it's just beyond the next corner of conversation, around the bend of mistrust or indifference.

Opening yourself up to others carries some form of risk. You can be disappointed or misunderstood; you can expect a lot and get a little. But what do we really risk in allowing ourselves easy interaction with others? The only ones who truly can bring heartfelt hurt into our lives are those whom we grow to love and count on. Even in these circumstances, we are provided with the capacity to forgive, and it is in our forgiveness that human imperfection is accepted.

Relationships should be treasured. We need to value them not as fool's gold that slips through our fingers but as if they were the rarest of gems. A famous Irish toast concludes, "And may God hold you in the hollow of his hand."

The nature of life and death is impossible to understand. Why should God need to hold some of us in the hollow of his hand when so many continue on this earth without faith or purpose? Yet that's the way the cards are dealt. So people must become our greatest treasure because we never know when those we love might be taken away from us.

I have seen people at their best when trying to help a blind person get along in the world. Even if their efforts are patronizing or misplaced, what must be decided is: Where are they really coming from? If the aid they offer is from the heart, even if the approach is somewhat demeaning or awkward, learn to accept the essential goodness offered in the intention.

Sharing

I believe we have developed an inherent mistrust of each other. We are weary, and when meeting someone new we usually do not let them know who we are or what we're really thinking. We posture and put up barriers, blocking honest interaction. Some of this is inherently necessary, in order to allow us to plug in our instincts so that we may assess the intent of the other person.

How many times have you been disappointed? If you're like me, it's impossible to count that high. As we work and compete to gain our life objectives, we fail more than we succeed.

All morning I sit at a computer or a piano trying to write something that others may think is valuable, as in the pages of this book. If my reason is for profit rather than purpose, I will inevitably fail. I must believe that I have something of value to say that may touch you and make a difference in your life. If the work is a bestseller, great. If only a few readers gain from the information contained in these pages, I'm still okay about it. I'm growing from the experience, and my capacity to understand who I am in the context of the world is becoming clearer and clearer. This is a reciprocal relationship, and our hope for the future hinges on whether we step across the barriers of indifference and embrace the concept of making a difference.

Find Your Gifts

Hal O' Leary has given his life in support of this idea. Born in Canada, Hal was raised in a family of hard work and relative affluence. It was the hope of his father and mother that he would enter the family business. But something inside said business wasn't for him.

In the late 1960s, Hal ran away from home and eventually migrated to Winter Park, Colorado—that wondrous ski town high in the Rocky Mountains. Hal was making a living as a ski instructor, enjoying the good life and not particularly interested in anything or anyone else. One morning, he was late for an instructors' meeting because he had been out the night before and overslept. Hal's boss had had enough and told him that he was being assigned to give ski lessons to a group of children coming up from Denver.

"Ah, come on," Hal said. "You know I don't deal with children very well."

His boss just smiled.

At the appointed hour, Hal was waiting outside the lodge at the base of the mountain when a bus pulled up and the driver opened the door. From inside, Hal heard the sound of children singing "100 Bottles of Beer on the Wall" and figured that these were pretty normal kids. So the shock on his face would have been obvious even to a blind person when the children started to disembark from the bus.

They were blind. And deaf. They were missing limbs, and suffered from spina bifida, epilepsy, brain damage, Down's syndrome, and other impairments. And in their midst was Reta Steadman, a woman with a mission.

One of the children had told Reta, a nurse at St. Joseph's Hospital, that her great dream was to ski, and to Reta, anything was possible. Ms. Steadman had been a trauma nurse in Vietnam. Having dealt with death, life problems seemed easily surmountable to this indomitable spirit.

"Are you O' Leary?" she said curtly, standing directly in his face.

"Yes, ma'am," Hal said, barely able to get the words out.

"Well let's go, O' Leary. Let's get this show on the road and teach these kids to ski."

"But how?" Hal blurted out.

"I don't know, O' Leary," Reta said, a slight smile creasing the corners of her mouth. "I suppose that's up to you."

Sometimes people meet purpose in a moment of epiphany. In Hal's case, it took a little while. By the third day, Reta and her children were under his care, and he had begun to imagine how specialized ski equipment might be fashioned, allowing amputees and other folks with disabilities the chance to begin to appreciate what it felt like to come down a beginner's slope unaided.

Two years later, Hal and Reta had become friends, and although Hal was still instructing in the regular ski program, more and more of his time was spent with these special-needs children. Then the bus started arriving without Reta, who simply left Hal a message that she was sick. He became worried enough to visit her in Denver and was shocked to learn that Reta Steadman, the rock, was suffering from an incurable melanoma.

Cancer eventually took her life. But over the next couple of years, Reta not only learned to ski as an amputee, she won the first world championships held in Colorado. Completely committed and inspired by the children and by Reta's life and death, Hal was determined to build the National Sports Center for the Disabled.

He didn't do this alone. The town of Winter Park got behind him, and some terrific people began raising money to create the appropriate foundation and serve on its board. The National Sports Center for the Disabled has taught well over a hundred thousand disabled people to ski. Its program is renowned worldwide, and has expanded to include other sports, such as rafting, hiking, and biking.

Hal O'Leary was looking for a purpose. He now changes the way the world looks at those with disabilities.

Grow Younger

If you're a television watcher, my friend Betty White has been in your living rooms, and, as she likes to say, sometimes your bedrooms, since you first watched a picture in black and white on a

12-inch screen. Betty has been a television fixture since 1950, when she began the first of fourteen TV series. It's obvious that many TV viewers have been in love with this Golden Girl, and my family is no exception.

It was Betty, in fact, along with her husband, Alan Ludden, who brought Patty and me together over thirty years ago. Betty and Alan had come to Cape Cod to do summer stock, the same year I had my first job playing piano and singing in a wonderful nightspot called Deacon's Perch in Yarmouthport. I was not only playing the piano, I was playing the field.

I can't say I was particularly discriminating—I simply was young and eager. Betty pointed out Patty Steffen, who was different from all the others. "It's in the eyes, Tom," she told me. "There's love in those eyes, and you'd better pay attention."

Thank goodness, I did. And thirty-three years later, Betty is the surrogate grandmother to our children, and has shared the authorship of a bestselling book with me called *The Leading Lady: Dinah's Story*, which chronicled the life of a remarkable guide dog and the effects she had on me and Betty. When Dinah was forced to retire, Betty stepped forward and added the dog to a house already full of loving animal friends. Betty is passionate about all creatures great and small, whether on four legs or two. A line from *The Leading Lady* sums it up. Betty wrote, "Dinah taught Tom to grow up, and Betty to grow old."

I know that there are people who are considered to be horse whisperers, but Betty's capacity to communicate with animals borders on the paranormal. I have seen her charm elephants and camels, giraffes and llamas. She is able to make eye contact with them and create a bond of trust. I'm very much an animal person, but I don't have a clue as to how she does it. Maybe it comes from something completely fundamental: Betty loves animals. Maybe it's that simple.

Love expressed honestly comes through even if we don't speak the same language.

Since it's public knowledge, it's okay for me to tell you that recently we celebrated Betty's eightieth birthday, a milestone in anyone's life. As we sat around the table, toasting and sharing stories with a group of her closest and dearest friends, I was not surprised by the love they expressed for her. What did shock me a little—and tickled my funny bone—was that when we were talking about the things we were doing, none of us had as many items on our plates as my friend Betty.

She's on the board of trustees of the Morris Animal Foundation, the largest funder of health studies for animals in the world; she serves as a board member of the Los Angeles Zoo; and, in her next book, she is chronicling the life and work of its animal keepers. She has found a new agent, is a commercial spokeswoman in great demand, and is even considering taking a part in another successful prime-time series. She's had a hip replacement and never lost a beat. She travels completely independently, carrying her bags so that she doesn't have to waste time at baggage claim when arriving at her destination.

Betty has a home in Carmel and drives up the California coast regularly, never tiring of the view. She is eighty years young, making a difference on behalf of animals and her friends. She has an unrivaled lust for life.

What are the stumbling blocks, the bumps in the road, the insecurities that get in the way of effective interaction across the human platform from one-on-one, group-to-group, race-to-race, and nation-to-nation? We must recognize the significance and, more importantly, the uniqueness found in all of us. We've all heard that no two people are exactly alike. And isn't that wonderful? Because it is in our differences that we discover the special buried treasure that is us.

There are more Good Samaritans in the world than there are Mr. Hydes. There are more people willing to go the extra mile on behalf of a stranger than there are those who lack compassion. At times of disaster and national crisis, we see people coming to the aid of strangers, providing enormous levels of economic support and love.

Our problem in connecting is actually more critically manifested in our unwillingness to deal with each other one-on-one. Teachers give up on students who they consider to be recalcitrant or difficult. Parents favor one child over another without taking the time to find the gifts that may be hidden in a child they don't understand. In relationships, couples forget why they fell in love, confused by the pressures put upon them by everyday life.

Judging people by a first impression limits your appreciation for beauty that might be found just below the surface. So how do we change the human model of interaction?

- Be willing to take risks.
- Take a chance on someone.
- Place yourself on the line and believe that the rewards will be worthwhile.
- Understand that even in the failure of a relationship, life lessons are learned.

The alternative is alienation and human anarchy—possibilities that I don't even want to consider. The truth is, I love people. I intend to keep on loving them, because I believe we are the most unique of all Creation's creatures.

Seeing Lessons Reflections and Exercises

How often have you heard people say that their second marriage is far richer than their first? Why? Because the couple has grasped the pitfalls of coupledom and worked to appreciate each other and avoid the negatives that brought about marital collapse.

If you think of people as gifts wrapped in different-colored paper, presented in different boxes, and tied up in different ribbon, you can become excited if you think of the joy that's possible in unwrapping a present. It's Christmas, everybody, and people are that special gift selected just for you. Open your heart and mind to the unlimited possibility of the interaction with others that's available. You'll find that:

- You'll become more cooperative.

- You'll expand your capacity to trust.

- You'll learn to appreciate the little things that make someone else unique and special.

- The qualities you possess are valuable to someone else.

- Love given is given back, in large measure; it is reciprocal, because our interaction is fundamentally based on appreciation and, as I noted earlier, our mutual interdependence.

Live with Purpose

This is our purpose: to make as meaningful as possible this life that has been bestowed upon us; to live in such a way that we may be proud of ourselves; to act in such a way that some part of us lives on.
—OSWALD SPENGLER

Who Are You Going to Be?

I bet we all remember telling our friends what we were going to be when we grew up. I explained to my cousin, Patricia, that I intended to become a great surgeon, never considering that a blind guy with a scalpel might present a significant danger to his patients. Then I went through a period when I thought I would become the next Clarence Darrow, an attorney standing before the bar of justice, arguing cases with the clarity of logic, bombastic veracity, and aplomb.

When my heart was broken by the first love of my life, I told my mother that I was prepared to become a priest and live as a monastic celibate. And then there were the moments I dreamed of playing centerfield for the Boston Red Sox. When it came to early purpose, it's fair to say that I was all over the lot. When considering my adult life, I'm not sure that I've changed very much.

When my son, Tom, was a senior in high school, he was asked to write an essay on the role his father played in his life. Obviously, part of what he wrote dealt with his perception of what I did for a living. With characteristic casualness, my son wrote, "My father is a singer, actor, athlete, author, humanitarian, community activist and a businessman. I'm not sure what he really does, but people like him, and they pay him."

You get the idea. I have been somewhat aimless in my commitment to a focused sense of purpose. This is not to say, however, that I haven't been intense when pursuing a goal. But it is not the same as the kind of application I've observed with many people throughout my life.

Life's Purpose

In 1968, I was a junior attending Harvard in Cambridge, Massachusetts. To earn money to pay for my tuition, I had begun singing in restaurants and clubs around the Boston area. One of my first great jobs was at a restaurant called Tallino's. The owner became a great early supporter of my career, and one night he told me that the actor Jack Lemmon was going to be having dinner in the dining room.

This was the first time a major star had ever heard me sing, and to say the least, I was pretty nervous. But Mr. Lemmon was great. He not only loved my performance, but I was shocked when he came up to the piano and suggested that he might sit in and play a little Gershwin.

He asked if I knew "Our Love Is Here to Stay."

"Sure," I said. "It's one of my favorite songs."

"What key, Tom?"

And just like that, Jack was accompanying a fledgling performer in a rendition of the Gershwin classic. The audience loved it, but nowhere near as much as I did.

Over the next two hours, Lemmon regaled me with show business stories dating all the way back to when he had attended Harvard and was a member of the Hasty Pudding Club, putting on shows in drag. At the end of the night, I remember floating back to my dorm, believing that I had made a new friend. After thirty years, I don't have any illusions, and I understand that for Jack Lemmon that evening was a small moment in a public and busy life. Yet the night set me on a course to chase my show business dream.

Eight years later, in the summer of 1976, I was cast in the forgettable movie *Airport '77*. Remember that during that time some big-budget movies dealt with natural disasters: *Earthquake*, *The*

Poseidon Adventure, Airport; my first screen credit was as a blind pianist in the Universal sequel to *Airport.*

One of the secrets in the success formula of these B movies was to put major stars by the dozens in the flick, and so it was that Jack Lemmon was cast as the doomed plane's pilot. I was so excited to be around such stars as Jimmy Stewart, Olivia de Havilland, Joseph Cotten, George Kennedy, Lee Grant, Kathleen Quinlan, and more.

The first person who made it a point to greet me on the first day of principal photography was Jack Lemmon. He not only remembered me, but I was shocked to find out that he had followed my career over the last nine years. He introduced me to everyone on the set as if he were a proud relative.

When we would show up in the mornings for makeup, I was astounded by Jack's energy. He was always the first actor on the set, and he was always willing to run lines with his fellow thespians, believing that you could never be too prepared for a scene. He loved his craft and believed that there could be magic in every moment placed on the screen. He was tireless in his desire to get it right. There was so much purpose in the way he did everything that we all picked up on his energy.

I'll never forget working with Kathleen Quinlan, having to perform a death scene, although I had never been in a movie before. When the plane crashed into the ocean, the piano was to topple over and crush me under its weight, killing me. Before I died, Jack asked me if I was prepared. "I guess so," I said. "I know the lines, and I think I understand the motivation of the character." He took me off to the side and worked with me for an hour, honing my rhythm and timing, talking about my motivation, giving me a clinic in Method 101.

At the end of my scene, everyone applauded, and I felt absolutely wonderful. I was sure I had died with dramatic glory. As the applause ended, I noticed that Jack and Jimmy Stewart were standing on the side of the set laughing uproariously. My confidence was completely shattered.

"Was something wrong?" I asked. "Did I mess the scene up?"

There are moments in show business that a fellow comes to treasure. Jimmy Stewart, in that stuttering delivery that only he could give, looked at me and said, "You know when you died, kid?"

"Yessir," I answered.

"Well—well, when you died, you were the first actor to ever do it with a smile on your face."

That's right: I died smiling. As a blind person, I had no sense of facial expression. When you pull out that old movie chestnut, *Airport '77*, you'll see an actor meeting the Grim Reaper with a smile on his face.

Over the next twenty years, Patty and I were fortunate enough to run into Jack at fund-raisers, screenings, award shows, or other show business events. He not only couldn't have been warmer during these encounters, but I was always amazed by the number of projects that seemed to be on his plate. From stage to film, he worked nonstop. This major star truly loved his craft.

The last time we were together was about six months before his death. I was hosting the Tom Sullivan Blind Children's Center Celebrity Golf Classic at Riviera Country Club. The tournament raises money for blind kids and their families, and I've been blessed to have wonderful celebrities participate. Over the years, Jack had been part of our day whenever he could, and I was delighted when I learned that he would be with us.

Over lunch, I sensed a change in him. He was weak, even feeble. His speech was soft, his step was slower, and I remember telling Patty later in the afternoon that I was really worried about him.

You all know the end of this story. We lost this national treasure through the ravages of cancer. But on that day as we ate lunch, what he talked about, with all of us enthralled, was the part he was going to play in a television movie titled *Tuesdays with Morrie.*

He was so excited, and I couldn't have been happier for him. As he was leaving, I told him how much I was looking forward to seeing his performance. "My purpose in taking this role, Tom," he said quietly, "is to bring dignity to death." How incredibly profound was this statement from a man preparing to face his own mortality. Jack Lemmon was not just focused on his purpose—he was *purposeful* in his commitment to his craft.

Finding My Calling

When my son described me as a fellow with a whole bunch of jobs, he was right. I have created and been involved in a number of careers. An agent once joked that I was the highest-paid recording artist who never had a hit record, and I hate to admit that he might be right.

I exploded onto the music scene in the late 1970s with tremendous hype. Unlike today, at that time a record career could be driven by all of the television talk shows that gave performers an outlet to bring their material directly to the public. From 1976 to 1980, I probably did fifty *Tonight Show*s with Johnny Carson and fifteen or twenty *Dinah* shows with the wonderful Dinah Shore. I cohosted for two weeks with Mike Douglas and was often seen on Merv Griffin. Along with all of that, I sang as a part of most of the acting jobs I did. I also toured with Shirley Bassey in Japan and was the opening act in Vegas for stars such as Danny Thomas, Liza Minelli, Don Rickles and Helen Reddy, to name a few. I did concerts on my own all over the country in theaters large and small.

So why did I end up moving on to a second career? Because

when all was said and done, as I laid in bed late at night tossing and turning and working to face my own reality, the truth was that I didn't really want it enough.

I hated the road. It was grueling traveling by bus, train, and plane with musicians from gig to gig. I found it incredibly boring. You get to the city, try to catch some sleep, set up for a sound check, eat bad food, give the performance, talk to the press, party too much, then lie down and go to sleep, hoping you'll have enough energy to do exactly the same thing the next day, all the while your family is growing up at home without you. I disliked the jive of the business, the glad-handing and backstabbing. And most of all, I hated the drugs that some people in the business were involved with.

I loved being a songwriter, and I loved being in the studio working with gifted producers and players to create a product I could be proud of. But the rest of the business placed a horrible strain on my marriage to Patty and demanded that I become something I wasn't. I simply didn't fit any of the profiles of an artist, at least not the stereotypes.

So when the chance came to work for *Good Morning, America* in 1978, I jumped at it. I was still forced to travel most of the time, but I was using all of my best qualities to create good television. My job, in a nutshell, was to bring inspirational stories from around the world to *GMA*. The story might be about a person with a disability overcoming the odds or a person doing something remarkable to benefit others; maybe an athlete on the comeback trail or an actor participating in a worthy nonprofit cause. Whatever *GMA* sent me to do offered incredible challenges and a wonderful sense of personal fulfillment, as we worked to bring great inspirational stories to the 7:45 A.M. time slot every Thursday for five years.

But even here, my purpose wasn't completely fulfilled, because I learned early on that I would never be given a chance to hold a permanent anchor position. That was not going to happen to a talent who was blind.

In 1983, facing the burnout factor, I had to move on to another career: movie production. In 1983, my autobiography, *If You Could See What I Hear,* was turned into a highly successful movie. All of my talents were focused and purposeful during that time. I not only wrote most of the music for the film but participated in the script with writer, director, and friend Stuart Gillard. I also coached actor Marc Singer in the nuances of playing me and was completely involved in every decision relating to marketing and publicity for the project.

Although this was only one movie, I knew from the first day that it was the kind of work I loved to do. But movies don't come along often, and I had to make a living. The success of *If You Could See What I Hear* prompted my entrance into the college and corporate lecture market. From 1983 to the present, I have spoken in over thirty countries and criss-crossed every state in the United States at least twenty times. It's a brutal grind but worth it when one person comes up to you backstage, hugs you, and says that you've made a difference in his or her life. This is the moment when purpose becomes purposeful, when a feeling of well-being flows over you because you know you've touched someone else's.

In *A Christmas Carol,* Ebenezer Scrooge was committed to making money. Greed was his god and profit was his only purpose. Yet through his encounters with the ghosts of Christmas past, present, and future, he learned to look outside himself in order to find his personal purpose. Tiny Tim taught him that giving was an essential part of living, and he changed his fundamental sense of priorities before it was too late.

Through the writing of books like this, my life as a lecturer, the music I've composed, the people I've learned from and those I've been able to help, the roles I've performed and the stories I've brought to television, my life is rich in its purpose, although that purpose is not necessarily singular in its focus.

The bottom line is that it comes down to whether we are purposeful in our efforts and whether our intention is to benefit others. I have never known anyone whose purpose was simply the accumulation of stuff. The stuff of life is acquired through hard work, diligence, and the gaining of personal wealth, but the substance that keeps the whole thing on an even keel is the need all of us share to be valuable to others. *Our purpose is to be purposeful.*

Some of us are more singular in our purpose to excel, and I've often heard it said that life is a lot easier for those who know exactly what they want to achieve. But I'm happy to be a member of the eclectic brotherhood who wake up every day hoping to find new challenges that provide purpose and make life purposeful.

Spiritual Purpose

My running partner on most early mornings in Palos Verdes, along with Partner, my German shepherd guide dog, is my spiritual counselor and friend, Clayton Cobb. Clayton is a Presbyterian minister at St. Peters-by-the-Sea, a beautiful church sitting on the cliffs above the Pacific that he has molded into a marvelous religious community.

On a recent morning jog, I asked him when he first discovered his calling to Christ. He said something like this: "I was in my second year of college, Tom, and I took a job in Hollywood working with teenage youth. By the end of that summer, the light burned in my soul, and as the Bible says, the way was clear. I knew without any shadow of a doubt that I wanted to serve God and become a shepherd to the flock."

Now that I think about it, he didn't say it quite that stiffly. But his commitment was obvious even as we struggled up a steep hill. What was even more interesting as the discussion continued was for me to learn how disappointed he is every time he feels that he's not reaching his parishioners. My friend agonizes over every Sunday sermon not because he's not eloquent—he's a tremendous preacher from the pulpit—but because he's working so hard to find just the right turn of phrase that will touch his audience. He's often explained that when he does not connect to a person in trouble, it is crushing to his sense of purpose.

I've observed the same disappointment when I talk to a surgeon who loses a patient or a teacher who can't reach a student. Most of these people knew early on what they wanted to be, so their investment in success and achievement is even more intense and purposeful than that of the eclectic.

People burn out because their purpose is too singular in its focus. You need to always take life seriously, but you can't get mired in individual failures. You may find yourself depressed as your purpose collides with the practical realities that beset all of us. So you must always keep your eyes on the prize. I've given depression a lot of thought because I really believe that you can't succeed in a purposeful way unless you have a handle on how to cope with disappointment.

Off the top of my head, I would guess that success and disappointment run about fifty-fifty on the life scale, so it's critical for each of us to figure out how to cope with both failure and depression. I have never experienced a moment of failure that didn't act as a guidepost placing me on the road toward the next success. The word *no* really means *not now. Never* is a word I will not allow to creep into my consciousness.

Other than those people who are clinically diagnosed with depression, I believe that depression is based on yesterday's news, not today's events. It is foolish to be depressed about a past experience. You cannot bring it back. You can only be depressed about the moment you're in, and once it's gone, it becomes yesterday's news. Learn from it, grow from it, evolve from it, be touched and changed by it, and figure out that life is a continuing process of expansion. If you are purposeful in your efforts, you will never be last in the pursuit of your goals.

This Hour, This Day

While writing *If You Could See What I Hear* with Derek Gill, my friend introduced me to Dr. Victor Frankl. Along with Sigmund Freud, Alfred Adler, and Carl Jung, Frankl led the early twentieth century renaissance into the human psyche. Victor Frankl's life circumstance prompted him to develop a concept he called *logotherapy*—therapy of the now.

If someone were to ask me what book has had the most profound effect on my life, without any hesitation I would say Frankl's *Man's Search for Meaning*. In it he describes the brutality he experienced in a concentration camp during World War II. Not only was he forced to watch his wife and children tortured, but he endured beatings, hunger, and work camps of incalculable cruelty. Yet through all of it his spirit lived in the moment of the now.

His purpose was this hour, this day, these months and years.

Frankl understood that at some basic level we do the best we can with who we are and what we have in each passing experience. When I met him at Derek's home for lunch, I was honored to learn that he had read *If You Could See What I Hear*.

"You, Mr. Sullivan," he boomed in his heavy Austrian accent from across the table, "fulfill the ultimate existential concept of my theory. You are a complete glass-half-full human being whose purpose is to get the most out of every life experience, interactive in the process and in love with your fellow man."

"You mean that I'm a purposeful person?" I asked timidly.

"That's right," he cried. "We can be deprived of everything, but if we remain purposeful, we are unbowed and undaunted. We will take risk. We will accept challenge. We will never be defeated by the negative. We will accentuate and extend the positive to every person we meet. We will live life to its fullest."

Defining our purpose is our life's mission, but recognizing the need to accept change and be flexible is the bottom line in the formula of purposeful success.

So be a person of purpose, and be purposeful in the attempt.

If you're consistent and willing to risk, you stand prepared to apply the action piece necessary to move forward. You will achieve the ultimate reward.

What stops us from being purposeful in our pursuit of goals? What are the factors that get in the way of personal achievement? We struggle when our vision is too narrow. Whatever we are pursuing, we must dream it, see it, and be it.

Fantasy is not as impractical as the concept implies. It finds its essential base in reality. In order for any of us to fantasize, we must have experienced a series of events that allows us to imagine what we can become.

Seeing Lessons Reflections and Exercises

You can't fulfill purpose without a commitment to persistence. I think the Bible is right: "Knock and it will open; seek and you shall find." Persistence commits you to the most important operational factor in fulfilling purpose: you have to keep trying and trying and trying.

We've all heard that success is 90 percent perspiration and 10 percent inspiration. I think the number may be skewed a little bit too much toward perspiration, but it isn't very far off. A purposeful process must set out both short-term and long-term goals, if purpose is ever going to be achieved. Without short-term benchmarks, you can easily become depressed over the day-to-day struggle to just get there. You also must accept failure as part of the purpose quotient. But the key to coping with these moments of trial and error is in reminding yourself that every negative can be turned into a positive.

I love talking to people who are fulfilled in their purpose. There's a sense of peace about them, a contentment with how they fit inside their own skin. They always seem to be in balance. But what about the people who are rudderless, purposeless, drifting on a sea of indifference? How do we touch them? How do we motivate them? How do we bring them more fully into the community?

A lot of us ask these questions. Teachers wonder how to teach. Parents ask how to reach their confused children. Employers wonder how to motivate workers who don't seem to take any interest in the growth or future of the business. The formula is really simple: *place value on their contributions.*

All of us want to believe that we are valued by someone else, and most of what we search for in becoming purposeful has to do with the recognition we are attempting to gain.

- If teachers recognize the smallest accomplishment in their student, they win.

- If parents celebrate each step of growth, children feel better about themselves.

- If an employer stimulates accomplishment, the company grows and employees begin to thrive as purposeful members of the community.

I'm amazed at how focused and purposeful a company can be, or a school system, or a health care program, or a community when people have a vested interest in the result. Cooperation leads to collaboration, which leads to achievement beyond what might have been possible for any of us acting alone.

Live with Passion

As life is action and passion, it is required of a man that he should share the passion and action of his time, at the peril of being not to have lived.
—OLIVER WENDELL HOLMES JR.

Golf as a Passionate Process

As the car turned right and made its way along winding Magnolia Drive, I rolled down the window and was embraced by a potpourri of delicious sensory treasures: magnolia, lilac, Georgia pine, roses, forsythia, along with fresh-cut grass. The medley of fragrances played in concert with the sounds of robins, orioles, pheasant, and the cry of a hawk diving for wild game. I was not arriving at some kind of hunting lodge or preserve, but what was preserved in this place was sacramental to those who come. I was going to challenge my skill and experience golf's nirvana.

I had been invited by friend and member Fleming Norville to play golf's Valhalla: Augusta National, home of the Masters in Augusta, Georgia. Bobby Jones said that it was his goal to build a golf course that would offer a full examination paper to test the mettle of professionals and amateurs alike. And here I was, a blind person, being given the chance to play Amen Corner. Striding over the Sarazen Bridge, I was reminded that Gene Sarazen had struck the five wood heard around the world. From approximately 240 yards away, this prodigious shot went into the hole, giving Sarazen a double eagle two that allowed him to go on and win the first Masters.

I was staying on the grounds in one of the Masters cottages, listening to the night sounds of whippoorwill and mockingbird, and becoming more nervous as I considered the exciting opportunity that awaited me in the morning. I had dinner in Augusta's beautifully appointed dining room and experienced a wine list unrivaled anywhere in the United States. The tables were full of members in green jackets and their guests: captains of industry, publishing magnates, politicians, and a few PGA pros sharpening their games for that year's tournament. Middleton Irish whiskey, convivial conversation, a steak that melted in my mouth, wondrous French burgundy, and bootlegged Havana cigars made the evening one I will never forget. Sleep? That was simply impossible.

I tossed and turned and dreamed, imagined, and most of all worried about the following day. Then it was there and we were headed for the driving range and a chance to warm up, wondering what the golf gods would bestow on this special day.

In preparation for the round, I had been practicing as if my very life depended on it. My hands ached from having hit hundreds of golf balls the previous weeks. I felt like my swing was in a good place, but when I began my warm-up with short chip shots, I found that I was taking the club back faster than I was swinging it at the ball. Come on, I told myself. Calm down. Get your nerves together. You've waited all of your life for this opportunity. Now make the most of it. Let your passion come out.

"What's the matter?" my friend and coach, Joe Assel, asked as I stood seemingly frozen on the driving range. "Oh nothing," I said. "I've just been thinking." "Well come on," he encouraged. "Let's keep working. They're going to be calling us to the tee very soon."

Whoops—there went my stomach. What was that I had for breakfast, a ham and cheese omelet? They never taste as good coming up as they do going down. Oh brother. Come on, Tom. Remember your passion. What's the worst that could happen? I could be embarrassed. I could play badly. But in the scheme of it all, so what? I was on Augusta National. Arnold Palmer had stood right here before he won the 1961 Masters. Jack Nicklaus had prepared for his assault on Augusta, hitting balls from this very spot. And more recently, Tiger Woods had thrilled the crowds as he warmed up with tee shots, flying the length of the driving range. So get a grip, Sullivan. Enjoy your passion.

I started to get in the groove. The next twenty shots I hit with various clubs, including those with the driver, rocketed off the club-face, flying on the intended line and finding the target. I heard the sonorous voice of the starter over my shoulder, not on a micro-phone, as on most courses—he was talking directly to my host, Fleming Norville. "You're on the tee whenever you're ready, Mr. Norville," he said. "By the way, we have rather heavy play this morning, so if it's all right with you, you will begin your round on the back side."

"Fine," my host said. "The back would be fine, Charlie."

No, it wouldn't, I thought, almost objecting out loud. Don't start me on the television holes. Ten, a par four, downhill—if you push it right, up in the pine straw, you're dead. Eleven, another par four, long, uphill, with a large bunker to the right of the green that eats golf balls, the beginning of Amen Corner. And then twelve, the toughest short par three in the world, over Raised Creek, the place where Tom Weisskopf took fourteen strokes to complete the hole; the place where Arnold Palmer took eleven, hitting three into the water. And then thirteen, the uphill par five, with the meandering Raised Creek still to contend with. And all of that was just the beginning. Here I was, blind, starting on the TV holes. Oh God, I could taste my omelet again.

As we walked toward the tenth tee with my legs feeling rub-bery, I tried to relax by telling my host how grateful I was to be there. "Thomas," he told me, "that's just what Bobby Jones said, that he never got tired of playing Augusta, because there was always a new challenge, something unique to learn, even at the end of his life. He described his feelings for this place as passionate."

We will only dare to risk if we can summon up our passion and learn to appreciate the moment.

And so in a flash of awareness that's exactly what I was determined to do. I was going to appreciate every moment of my

Augusta experience. If I missed a shot, so what? If I hit a ball into Raised Creek, I would take another one out of my bag and try again. I would appreciate the lilac and dogwood and not allow anything to get in the way of a once-in-a-lifetime moment.

For the first six holes, I played the finest golf of my life. On ten, I hit a big-time tee shot, right in the middle of the fairway—not as long as Tiger, but not short either. A second shot put me in the bunker in front of the green, but I exploded out beautifully, missed a putt for par, and made what for me was a sensational bogey. I parred eleven, with two career shots and a smooth two putt.

And then there I was, standing on the twelfth, the daunting par three over Raised Creek. The warm, caressing zephyr was blowing at five to eight miles an hour in our faces. What should it be for me—a seven iron, an eight iron, or a hard nine? I opted to hit a smooth seven, and never in my life had I ever struck a Titleist so precisely. The ball flew just over the flag and landed twenty feet behind the pin on the back edge of the green. That was terrific!

The problem was, from there the putt was straight downhill. Players in the Masters had often literally putted it off the frontage of the green into Raised Creek. How would I do? I remember the caddy saying, "Just touch it, Mr. Sullivan. Just touch it."

Thank God, blind people can muster just that kind of feathery stroke. My putt barely lipped out of the hole and stopped less than a foot below, making the tap-in par routine. *Wow.*

Now we were on the thirteenth, and I was so pumped up I bogeyed the par five. Going on, I bogeyed the next par four and capped off my six-hole bonanza with a par on the extraordinary par five fifteenth. Let me hasten to tell you that Augusta, as she always does, took back all of my good shots. The rest of my day was ho-hum golf—some good, some bad. But my moments expressing passion in the Georgia sun, walking the same fairways as Player,

Nicklaus, and Palmer, committed me to the belief that none of us can live successful lives without the constant affirmation and appreciation of our individual passions.

Can You Be Too Passionate?

I have friends who would probably tell you that they think I'm too passionate about everything. "He can't be that enthusiastic about all the stuff he does," they would say. "It must be hype. Or he's just trying to convince himself that life is terrific." I can see where they're coming from. I certainly am an ebullient person, prone to flights of fantasy, exaggeration, and leaping before I look.

"So what!" I would tell them. "What's the worst thing that can happen when you follow your passion? You don't succeed." But to paraphrase a writer much brighter than I am, you can be noble in the attempt.

I'm sure most people would believe that a blind golfer could never play a decent round of golf on Augusta National. Well, they're wrong, just as the naysayers were proven incorrect in so many historic examples. I know people must have said, "They'll never get that thing off the ground" at Kitty Hawk, and sixty-six years later, "We just don't have the aerospace technology necessary to land a man on the Moon." Or "There's no vaccine for polio." Don't ever say never to a passionate person. He or she will prove you wrong at every turn. And passion is contagious.

Coaches motivate teams. A general rallies his troops. Corporate chairpeople with vision create standards of industrial excellence. Passion is persuasive. Politicians convince us that they know best. Pitchmen sell us products, and priests, pastors, and other clergy convince us that our faith will be rewarded.

In a real sense, passion is catching.

I was passionate about music from my earliest memory. I actually can remember lying in my crib with a bottle in my mouth listening to my grandmother sing me an Irish lullaby while she played on a spinet piano nearby. As soon as I could walk, I listened to the radio for hours on end, pounding on whatever I could get my hands on to create rhythm to the music. My mother had me singing in front of her friends by the time I was three, and my repertoire included everything from Irish ballads to Hank Williams country melodies. I wasn't just precocious—I was passionate about music of all kinds. Through high school and college I was a soloist for the choir, played in the orchestra, and spent almost every free moment jamming with my friends.

My passion has led to a wonderful musical career, from performing on every talk show on television during the '70s and '80s, to concert stages and nightclubs around the world. I wrote, recorded, sang, and lived my music. But often, we let our passion get sidetracked. In my case, it was when circumstances collided with opportunity. Through music I was invited to be a guest on ABC's *Good Morning, America,* and through a bizarre set of circumstances I ended up working for *GMA* as a principal correspondent for eight years. I was also acting on television series, making movies, and beginning to excel as a motivational speaker. All of these activities served as diversions from my musical passion. Before I knew it, I wasn't involved in music anymore.

At some point in the late '80s and early '90s, I realized that in describing myself I was no longer a singer, musician, songwriter; I had become an author, television personality, and motivational speaker. Not bad. But certainly not as satisfying.

Do not allow yourself to ever be pulled away from your passion. Don't be diverted or drawn off course. Stay in it for the long haul. You will be better off.

I very much regret not hearing the music played in my head anymore.

My Son and I

Although I still write and perform an occasional movie theme and sometimes work on other people's albums, music is no longer the centerpiece of my life. But passion is contagious and transferable. My son, Tom Sullivan Jr., is consumed by his passion for music, and it never really manifested itself until he was about twenty years old. I'm proud to say he has become an excellent musician with his own distinctive style. But I'm reminded as I write these pages of the first time I became aware of his musical talent.

My son was languishing in college. He had no academic interest and hated the idea that we had made him attend. In fact, during his sophomore year I don't really know if he went to class at all. But I do remember the day that he came home and asked me if I would listen to a cassette he had made of a new band. He said that they were a local bar group, but he thought they had real potential and wanted to know what I thought. As I listened, I wasn't impressed with the musicianship, but I thought that the songwriting was interesting. There was, however, one person who seemed to stand out from the rest. It was the bass player, and I commented to my son that I thought this guy could really lay down a good groove, his timing was impeccable, and he might have a future.

Even a blind person can hear the sound of a smile when it spreads over another's face. And I heard my son as he expressed a complete Cheshire cat grin.

"That's me, Dad," he told me. "I'm the bass player."

I couldn't believe it. "When did you begin studying the instrument?" I asked him, amazed.

"When I went away to college," he said sheepishly. "That's kind of what I've been doing up there."

I didn't have to be hit over the head with a hammer to understand that Tom needed to pursue his musical dreams. And so he continued at the music institute, and from day one, we saw his passion unleashed. He graduated with two degrees: one in performance and one in recording engineering. At this writing, he completed his first CD, called *Ride,* and his band Mushu Pie Train is really catching on.

During the making of the CD, he asked me if I would be interested in helping him write some arrangements for the horn section and backup singers. I poured my heart into the effort. Love and skill came together, and I really felt that I had done a great job on Tom's behalf.

At one of the recording sessions with some of the best sidemen in L.A., I got particularly excited when the horn section played a complex passage that I was really proud of. My son came over to me quietly. "Dad," he said, "you have to take those horns out."

"What?" I said rather indignantly.

"You have to take them out," he insisted.

"But Tom," I protested, "this is the best stuff on the album!"

My son paused, with an expression I'm sure was a mixture of hurt and concern. "Dad," he said carefully, "it's great stuff. But it's *your* stuff."

Thank God, I have achieved a maturity of character. "Okay," I told my son, "right away." And you know what? He was right. The music has now come full circle. The chain has not been broken. My passion for this wondrous art form has been passed on in melody, lyrics, and song to my son, who now does it far better than his father.

· · ·

A few years ago, I did a television pilot for a series called *Aaron's Way*, with Merlin Olsen, the great defensive tackle for the Los Angeles Rams during the mid-'60s. Being a pro football fanatic, I spent most of our free time trying to get Merlin to tell me stories about the game, its players, and the moments he remembered best. In the course of our conversation, I asked him if he had ever been injured severely. "Only once," he said, "and the worst part of it was that it happened in a game that didn't matter. It was late in the season, and we had already locked up the conference championship. Because I really wasn't involved in the action as I should have been, I was sort of working at half-speed and got clocked in the knee by an over-zealous rookie. Bam! That was it for my knee. The pain, the surgery, and the rehab wouldn't have occurred if I had been going at full speed."

"With passion?" I suggested.

"You bet, Tom," he told me. "If you're not passionate out there, you're going to get hurt."

Passions, Joys, Risks, and Rewards

Passion is the joyous celebration of our own uniqueness expressing itself with directed, purposeful energy. If we're not passionate about *all* of our life experiences, the only person who will pay the price is us. Passion is intensity, not work. It cannot be faked or forced. It's not a scattergun approach. It is directed. It's true that you can be a passionate person interested in many things. Leonardo da Vinci was an artist, an inventor, an architect, a musician, and more. But when designing or painting, he understood that his genius required focus.

Focus is a necessary part of applying passion to our lives. But how do we find our passion? And then, how do we learn to focus its energy?

We must not be afraid to fail. More success is lost, more challenges unmet, and more opportunities squandered when people are afraid to risk personal failure. During the first year I was learning to play golf, there were days too numerous to count when I heard the horrible sound of *whiff* as my club completely missed contacting the golf ball. Nothing can be more frustrating or exasperating, especially when it is followed by a patronizing teacher saying, "That's all right, Tom. Actually, it was a very good swing. Your club just passed over the top of the ball."

So what, I thought. Dammit. I wanted to hit the hell out of it, not miss it! But every day I returned to try again, not being put off by my failure and wanting my success more. This led to Augusta and so many moments with my playing partners and friends that have provided me with inestimable pleasure.

The concept of risk/reward connects directly to whether we are willing to take a chance and follow our *passions*. Note that I am using the plural passions. Singular passion can often lead to an imbalance in personality. Multipassions serve us better in defining our overall adjustment to life. Just as the law of science teaches us that energy can neither be created nor destroyed, passion finds its essence when experience serves as a catalyst, creating a feeling in the gut, a beating of the heart, and the release of an energy that is unstoppable.

I believe that most of us don't actualize our potential principally because we do not effectively release our passion. The fear factor holds us back. We also spend a great deal of time wondering how others will feel about our decision. Essentially, if a person is really a friend, he or she will always be supportive.

No winner has ever existed without giving bent to his passion, and no passion has ever taken us to our goals without connecting it to other people of like minds. There is a danger in the expression of passion that we can become selfish and self-involved. I know many people whose passion isolates them in their own pursuits. Frankly, some of this is necessary, because commitment and a work ethic go hand in hand with the expression of passion. But people who only project self-directed passion without considering their impact on others can often damage those around them, and in a larger context, affect communities, nations, and the world.

How do you find your passion? Embracing passion comes principally through trial and error. We can all point to starts and stops along the way and frustrations that made us wonder if we would ever really know what road to take.

The journey is fraught with pitfalls, but the top of the mountain makes any climb worthwhile. I've been privileged to know Eric Weinhemayer. He's the young blind man who recently climbed and conquered Mt. Everest. Twenty-nine thousand feet, give or take a few, and this astounding, passionate person achieved the goal without the benefit of sight. I have been an athlete all my life, but I cannot even imagine the physical toll and mental concentration necessary for Eric to have accomplished such an amazing feat. When I asked him why, he quipped, "Why not? I want to find out what a blind person can sense at the top of the world." And you know what? He knows. The reality is, he's the only blind person who will probably ever know. If it can be imagined, it can be achieved. As long as passion's energy is focused and the willingness to work and sacrifice drives our efforts, all of us can realize accomplishments we did not believe were possible.

Your Best Self

We often hear talk about the burnout factor. This is when someone has applied what is seemingly a passionate commitment to a job or purpose, then decided they he or she has had enough. I believe this occurs when the purity of passion is compromised with the need for acceptance or financial security. I have never met a person imbued with a substantial level of passion who ever burned out. It's true that it may be necessary to take a hiatus and move on to other things for a time, but you should never give up passion.

Essentially it is your passion that expresses your best self.

Passion can be seriously misunderstood. We all know people who have been so involved in doing something that they were rude, clipped, or distant when we tried to engage them in conversation. Although the brain can deal with a number of thoughts at the same time and we like to think that we are multitasking, we really complete only one job at a time.

What Helen Keller Taught Me

We all become aware of our passions when we are touched, motivated, or moved by the passion of someone else. The person who plugged me into the search for my passion was the remarkable Helen Keller.

In the Prologue I talked about having been honored with a Lifetime Achievement Award given in Ms. Keller's name by the American Foundation for the Blind. I was reminded that night of a childhood experience that greatly affected the course that my personal odyssey would take.

I was nine when the Perkins School for the Blind in Watertown,

Massachusetts, honored Ms. Keller on her eightieth birthday. There was to be a ceremony in our school auditorium when we would hear Ms. Keller speak and learn of her many achievements. That morning I had been late for my first class because some friends and I were playing loud rock-and-roll and never heard the bell ring. The principal was about to levy me with a punishment as Ms. Keller was escorted into his office. Somehow she learned that I was present and in trouble. I remember hearing her ask in her uniquely personal voice, "Why is this little boy in trouble?"

"He was late for class," the principal explained, "because he was off playing some of that boogie woogie rock-and-roll."

Ms. Keller's teacher finger-spelled what he said into her hand. And then I heard her laugh. "You mean, he's kind of a little devil. Are you a little devil, little boy?" she asked. Helen Keller was actually speaking to me! "No, ma'am," I said. "I just love music, and I guess we got carried away." Her response was amazing. "Good for you, boy. Good for you! Now, we don't want you to be late for class. But forever and ever and ever, keep pursuing your passion."

Even at this early age, I remember how I felt. I was released from the constraints of the system. Helen Keller had told me to pursue my passion, and that was exactly what I was going to do.

I will admit I probably have taken the concept of passionate pursuit a little too far in every segment of my life. From my career goals to the sports I pursue as a hobby, it's probably fair to say that I am over the top in the application of my passions. But frankly, I don't want it any other way. I am not ever going to compromise the engagement with the world that comes from the expression of passion. I will never master my passion because it is only in challenge that growth will occur.

Our passions engage us in the experience of being alive. They allow us to risk in order to gain reward. They come from our core and are the songs sung by our souls. If we deny them, we are less.

If we do not continue searching for them, we are far less than we were meant to be. They are not always obvious, yet each of us knows when we have discovered them. Hold your passions close to your heart, and as you embrace them, recognize that it is only in the expression of passion that life will find true meaning.

Seeing Lessons Reflections and Exercises

Passion is the catalyst, the additive, the chemical, the element, the thing that activates pride, connects us to people, and focuses us on our purpose. I designed these last four life secrets to be a synergistic combination of concepts, all interactive in their application, giving us a formula for living that guarantees the ultimate experience in what it means to be a successful human being.

Your individual success begins with evaluating what activity or goal may provide you with your own personal purpose. Determine to pursue your goals with pride by demonstrating the discipline to carry them out, through taking personal responsibility for individual daily effort. Clearly acknowledge that these goals cannot and will not be achieved without the recognition of the significance and the talents of other people, and kick the whole process up a notch by applying your passion without fear of failure.

This book is largely about the development of core values that will sustain you when life's storms toss and turn you on your dangerous individual ocean voyages. We are always looking for a safe harbor, a place where we are loved, nurtured, and protected by others. But you must be brave and courageous in the application of these values. Through pride, people, purpose, and passion, you have at your fingertips the principles that will allow you to face your fears directly and to turn to the operational structure you need to continue to grow and prosper.

Through the application of pride, recognition of people, and focus on your purpose, you can unleash your passion, galvanizing yourself into action. So no more sitting on the sidelines. No more glass-half-empty approach. No more hesitation when entering the game and accepting the challenges that are set before you. No more fear. No more doubt. Only an ebullience of spirit that allows you far greater success than even your own fantasies may have expressed.

I absolutely believe that none of us use even half of our potential to become the best possible. But with the application of pride, people, purpose, and passion as core philosophic values, I promise that your life will be enriched tenfold, and you will grow to be a far better person than you ever imagined.

Take a Second Look— Living with Labels

*I have a dream that one day this nation will rise up and
live out the true meaning of its creed: "We hold these
truths to be self-evident, that all men are created equal."*
—Martin Luther King Jr.

Life As Blindy

Until the day when I engineered my own escape, the backyard my parents confined me to was as much a prison as Alcatraz. Much like the Birdman, only allowed to look at the world through the tiny aperture of a window high up on the wall of his cell, I learned about life listening to its ebb and flow from behind the eight-foot chain-link fence.

My obsession was baseball, and the Boston Red Sox were my team. My fantasy was to play center field and share a World Series with the great number 9, Ted Williams. From the confines of my prison yard, I could hear the sounds drifting up the hill on a spring wind from the neighborhood school. Every day, boys filled the air with the crack of the bat and the sound of balls popping into people's gloves as they played the grand old American game.

I desperately wanted to be part of those games, but all I had was my radio with the Red Sox broadcast, along with rocks I picked up from the ground to use as baseballs and an old Louisville Slugger bat my father had given me.

As Curt Gowdey did the play-by-play, I announced my own games: "Now batting for the Boston Red Sox, number 8, Tom Sullivan. Sullivan's had a great season. He's hitting 325 on the year with 22 home runs and 61 runs batted in, and he's got quite a history against Yankee left-handed ace Whitey Ford. How will Whitey pitch to him? Let's see."

I bent down and picked up a rock, and held the bat over my right shoulder.

"Here's the windup and the pitch."

I threw the rock into the air and swung the bat, missing the rock completely.

"Strike one on Sullivan! Old Whitey really had him guessing on that curve ball. Let's see what he comes back with now. Here's the next one."

This time I made believe the ball was outside, letting the rock drop to the ground.

"Ball one outside! Whitey tempted him with a little heat, but Sullivan laid off that pitch. The count is one ball, one strike. Whitey's ready, and he deals."

Again, I threw the rock up in the air and swung the bat with all of my nine-year-old might. The crack of wood on a rock was fantastic to hear.

"It's a high fly ball deep into center field! Mantle going back, back, back, looking up, and that one is gone! A home run for Tom Sullivan, number 23 on the season, and the Red Sox lead the Yankees 1 to nothing!"

While all this was going on, someone was watching, but he wasn't a fan or a friend. He was a boy with a cruel heart. He stood outside my fence, and I'm sure if I could see his face I would have noted the smirk of derision that clouded it. The sound of his voice seemed almost matter-of-fact.

"What's the matter, kid?" he began. "Are you *blind*?"

"Yes," I answered. "I'm Tom Sullivan, and I'm blind," wanting to be honest.

"You're blind!" he chided. "And you're trying to play baseball. That's kind of *stupid*, isn't it?"

"Who are you?" I asked.

"Just a kid who thinks you're stupid."

And then he began a chant that I can still hear today: "Blindy, blindy, blindy, blindy, blindy, blindy, blindy, blindy, blindy, blindy, blindy, blindy."

In that moment, for the first time in my life I hated a human being. I picked up rocks from the ground, throwing them at him, trying to hit him, trying to kill him. He just ducked out of the way and kept on chanting.

"Blindy, blindy, blindy."

At some point he got tired of the game and went away, the sound of his voice fading from my ear but never from my mind.

I will be charitable and say that the boy who called me blindy was simply being insensitive and childish. His perception was that he was superior to me, and that by being able to categorize me with the label "blind" he was somehow better.

Labels and Ugliness

When we label others in a negative way, we are dismissing them and considering them unimportant in our perception of what constitutes a valuable human being. It could also be said that labeling others is a form of protectionism. If I place a label on you, I put myself in a position that allows me to apply categorical judgment on everything about you—your race, color, creed, and gender become convenient slots into which you fit.

Being blind has afforded me the opportunity to look behind the immediates of physical appearance and ethnicity. To repeat what I said earlier: I have never met an ugly person unless he or she wanted to be, unless he or she demonstrated a personality that was truly ugly in its manifestation.

Think about it:

- Cruelty for its own sake is ugly.

- Arrogance is ugly.

- Misplaced anger is ugly.

- Ethnic cleansing is ugly.

- Racial prejudice is ugly.

- Socioeconomic bigotry is ugly.

There are bad people in the world, and when we see the ugliness of human intolerance, we must do everything possible to stamp it out.

The Lessons of Music and Dr. King

As a teenager in the '60s, I must admit I was reflecting a certain ugliness. You could say that I had a chip on my shoulder. During the week, at the Perkins School for the Blind, I was usually the best at everything—best singer, best actor, best athlete, best student. But on weekends when I'd return to my neighborhood I was often the person no one would hang out with, particularly when I moved away from my friend, Billy Hannon.

While attending Perkins, my life was changed when I was blessed to have the opportunity to study piano with Henry Santos. Hank was not only a gifted classical pianist, but during his own college years he had played jazz in clubs, then in service bands while in the armed forces. He loved all forms of music and recognized early that the best way to motivate me to play Chopin was to make it fun.

He not only exposed me to the best of jazz but introduced me to gospel and encouraged me to attend predominantly black revival services in churches throughout the Boston area. So there I was, in heaven, as I joined the choirs singing "Jesus Walked that Lonesome Valley" and "We Are Climbing Jacob's Ladder." It was the first time somebody told me I had blue-eyed soul, and I considered that to be a badge of honor.

Hank didn't just work at my musical education; he mentored

my education in life. Better than most, he understood the chip on my shoulder and figured out that I had to be exposed early on to the teachings of Dr. Martin Luther King.

It happened that my teacher had been Dr. King's roommate while attending Boston University. I remember how amazed I was when Mr. Santos introduced me to many of King's letters written from a prison cell and speeches he had given while crisscrossing our country in the name of civil rights.

Eventually I had the opportunity to meet Dr. King, and I'll never forget how quickly he honed in on his perception of who I was. In a short time, he made me understand that the problem was not in others; it was in me. *I* was putting out the bad vibe. *I* was being intolerant. *I* had to change.

I came to understand that most people meant well, that they were not prejudiced—they were simply misinformed. I experienced a true catharsis of spirit. In this breakthrough, I grew to realize that love and respect, when expressed openly, can overcome almost all negative stereotyping.

You have to assess where a person is coming from in a social interaction. For example, very often people's efforts at kindness toward me could be perceived as condescending. In a restaurant, a waitress may look at our group sitting at a table and ask, "What would he like to eat?" Or someone else may believe that I need to be guided into a chair. Both approaches are rather humiliating, but the question I've come to ask myself whenever I face these occasions is, Where is the person coming from? Is he or she reacting out of real concern for my well-being?

Most of the time, people are acting in a caring manner. And as I've gotten older, I've learned to assess these awkward encounters fairly accurately. When I face people directly and explain quietly that I'm more capable than they might expect, they are generally quick to change their approach.

I will probably not live long enough to witness the elimination of people's condescension when dealing with my blindness. It is seemingly engrained in the makeup of certain individuals and it starts with something as basic as physical perception.

How shallow we are when determining our relationship to others based on our perception of physical beauty. What is sexy to one group in one part of the earth may be considered completely unattractive to another. Yet I am continually amazed at how surface-oriented we can be, and how easy it is for all of us to apply physical labels that carry over into judgments about a person's character: the dumb blonde, the glasses-wearing nerd, the happy fat man, the dumb jock.

What Muhammad Ali Taught Me

I came to understand the profound absurdity connected to physical labeling while working for *Good Morning, America.* One of my assignments in 1979 was to go to Deer Lake, Pennsylvania, and spend three days with the Champ, Muhammad Ali.

It's interesting about labels: When you apply "the Champ" to Muhammad, it fits perfectly. He is a champion in every way but much more so *out* of the ring. At the time I interviewed him, he was about to fight Larry Holmes in his effort to win the heavyweight championship of the world for the fourth time. All of the boxing pundits believed he was making a mistake entering the ring at age thirty-eight. History has proven that they were right. Doctors now say that Ali's Parkinson's disease was largely brought on by the pounding he took over twenty years in the fight game. But at the time we met, he sincerely believed he could once again regain the title and wear the championship belt.

Being the heavyweight champ, wearing that label, meant more to Muhammad than his health. He had been to the Mayo Clinic, where they had told him he was endangering not only his brain but his life. His longtime friend and physician, Dr. Ferdy Pacheco, had come out publicly decrying the Champ's continuing effort to fight. His trainer, Angelo Dundee, did everything possible to keep him from going into the ring. But Muhammad was committed to his own belief that he was the greatest.

And so there we were at Deer Lake, and even a blind man knew the Champ should not have been fighting. He wasn't doing his road work because he didn't feel good. He napped for hours. His trainers didn't let him spar; he just worked on the heavy bag. His speech was slurred, and though he talked a good game, I never really felt he believed in his own ability to beat Larry Holmes.

Most meaningful for me were our conversations off-camera about the world, Islam, faith, marriage, and family rather than fighting. Muhammad Ali is so much more than a fighter, but at the time I spoke with him being a fighter was the label that he considered important, so he risked everything and lost.

After the fight, Larry Holmes told the reporters, with tears in his eyes, that he never hit the Champ in the head. He just didn't want to hurt him. He pounded his body for eight rounds until the referee stopped it. Even in the violent world of pugilism, there was kindness. Holmes, a great champion himself, made it clear to everyone who would listen that Muhammad Ali was the greatest fighter of all time and that he was sorry they had met under these conditions.

Over the years, I've run into Muhammad on airplanes or at events, and what strikes me now is how content he seems to be with his lot in life. He told me that he ministers to the world and lives the tenets of Islam with a profound commitment to peace. I not only believe him but embrace his calling. He is a human treasure not because of a great left jab and the ability to move in the ring with a fluidity never seen before or since in a boxer but because of who he is—a man of faith and love.

Beauty and the Blind Guy

In show business they call it reading your own press—that is, when you are dubbed "beautiful" and you believe it. However, sometimes seeing is not believing and beauty is experienced on a far deeper level. *Good Morning America* sent me on assignment to interview Bo Derek, the young actress who was dubbed the perfect 10 in the movie *10*.

A lot of guys thought it was really stupid for ABC and *Good Morning, America* to send a blind correspondent to interview Bo Derek. They thought it made no sense to waste this time with Bo on a guy who couldn't see the perfect 10. What they didn't figure out was that I might just have a different approach to the interview. And I did. And it was one of the most important interviews I ever conducted during my tenure at *Good Morning, America*.

So here we were, Beauty and the Blind Guy, sitting on a contrived set meant to look like a ranch landscape. My approach to the conversation, as usual, came to me while showering earlier that morning. I decided to put it right on the line, coming right out of the box, so I began with this question:

"Bo," I said, "my friends tell me you're a perfect 10, but since I can't see you, why should I think you're interesting or beautiful on the inside or that you're a person who could teach me something?"

Twenty years later, I am still wondering what went through Bo's mind when she heard the question. Did she think I was being flippant or fresh? Did she believe it was a trick question? Or, did she think I simply was insensitive or crazy? To her great credit, Bo Derek reacted with real sensitivity.

First, she began to cry. And then she enlightened me and my morning audience. "Tom," she said, "that's the problem. Nobody looks beyond the immediates of their perception of who I am. They see me as this physical person and never take the time to be interested in what I think or feel, or how I can be hurt by the cruelty of the press."

Now *I* was really surprised. The young woman who seemingly had it all was saying that she wanted to be appreciated for so much more than physical attributes. She told me of her love for animals and her concern for the environment. She talked about the importance of her marriage and her desire to see and appreciate the world. There was a solid brain ticking inside that beautiful head, and it needed to be appreciated and respected.

Thanks, Bo, for reminding me that none of us are exactly as we seem. We have myriad complexities, and we all search to find the balance between the perception of others and our own reality. I suppose the balance in our labels we're all trying to reach for comes down to whether we're comfortable in our own skin.

I don't think I was able to celebrate my own uniqueness until I got over worrying about the way others saw me. I've learned to make being blind a positive, and I've even embraced the idea that sometimes I can turn this disability into a marvelous asset.

Dropping the system of labels will break down the barriers that separate us from becoming a homogeneous society. Your ethnic heritage is something to be proud of. But this chapter is about digging deeper. The goal is to stretch past the immediates, to take the time and understand the specialness that has been given to each of us, and to recognize that if we label each other, we label ourselves. *We* become bigoted, *we* become prejudiced, and, most important, we miss the opportunity to know someone who may enhance our lives.

There is no risk in putting aside the system of labels—there's only reward. It's true that we all have to work harder to really get to know someone. But I'm convinced it's worth the effort. Some of my most important relationships have come when my first impression was proven wrong. Going with your gut really means opening your heart. Taking a second look is often the key that opens the lock to friendship, our most important treasure.

Labels and Global Crisis

The videotape showed Osama Bin Laden and his followers gathered in a room somewhere in Afghanistan watching CNN's coverage as airplanes ripped into the World Trade Center and the Pentagon. At each cataclysmic, catastrophic crash, Bin Laden raised his hands in praise to Allah. "Allah be praised," the translation noted. "May Allah's will be done." Almost three thousand lives lost in the Trade Center, hundreds in the Pentagon, and hundreds more on the doomed aircraft, all in the name of Allah.

Is it a phenomenon of this moment in history? Sadly, it is not. In God's name, men have been killing men as far back as recorded time. The Crusades, in God's name, cost millions of Christian and Muslim lives. The Inquisition, in God's name, tortured and murdered innocent human beings over their faith. Fourteen million Jews were eliminated by the Nazis in the name of racial purification. Bible Belt thumpers hanged blacks throughout the South, and millions of other black men and women were enslaved by whites who believed it was acceptable to own another human being.

I voiced all of these feelings to my friend, Clayton Cobb, as we ran on the morning of September 11, 2002, one year following the tragedy. I asked him why civilized men and women create acts of atrocity and human cruelty in God's name.

Minister Cobb is very wise, and he provided me with an answer I had never considered before. "Tom, it's because we—mankind—are always remaking God's image in our likeness, rather than recognizing we must exist in the image of God." And here we come to the fundamental basis for racial profiling and prejudicial labeling. If you don't look like me and act like me and live like me, you're not equal to me, and I am superior to you in every way. Labeling allows us to stay in our own comfort zone, never having to be disquieted in our interaction with others. I am so grateful that blindness has taught me to look beyond the immediates, because the gifts that I've received, allowing people to reveal their true nature over time, have been incomprehensibly valuable and beautiful.

Seeing Lessons Reflections and Exercises

There are benefits in wearing your labels proudly and declaring them openly, because in your declaration you force yourself to live up to the model you believe yourself to be. The psychology of label responsibility is a powerful driving force that engenders both confidence and commitment to your own and other people's perceptions of who you are.

Living your label does not mean posturing it, or posing it, or, maybe even better said, imposing it on others. Living your label relates directly to taking responsibility for it and embracing it as only one very important part of your persona. To categorize who you are according to your labels places all kinds of expectations on you. Consider these examples:

- The great athlete who retires and suffers because he is no longer in the public eye

- The businessman who is so focused on his corporate success that he loses connection to his family

- The gay person, black person, or disabled person who places labels so far out in front of everything else, then suffers because others cannot get to know the true colors of his or her heart

Labels place a limit on your capacity for intimacy, because they block exposing your inner self. When you eliminate your vulnerability by the posturing of your labels, you limit your ability to understand not only where I'm coming from but to love me unconditionally. Appreciating our differences a positive application of labels. My appreciation for the world I inhabit as a blind person allows me to bring you into that world and expand your appreciation for the other four senses.

The pride you feel in your ethnicity exposes me to its history and makes me a more well-rounded human being. My appreciation for your background, your religion, moral positions, sexual orientation, and family commitments broadens my appreciation for who you are and how you choose to live.

My ability to be open-minded when dealing with you comes from your capacity to adopt your label wisely and not place me in a circumstance where I am forced to wrap you only in the veil of your label. I do not have the right to ridicule by trying to rework you into what I believe to be an appropriate image and likeness of myself; neither should you limit my ability to know you by posturing a label that allows you to hide behind the impenetrable wall built by your own insecurity.

Tear down the walls. Throw away the fears. Open your hearts. Experience true love that can only be expressed by taking a risk in order to know, in order to grow. I am no better or worse than you, but I am less than you if I am not open to the possibility of being able to say easily, openly, and without constraint, "I love you."

- Change the construction of your labels in the decisions you make, defining appropriate label choices.

- Value substance above style in all things.

- Orient your thinking to value and character, rather than characterizing yourself according to physical attributes or external beauty.

- Don't make snap judgments or have instant reactions that allow the uniqueness of people to get lost.

- Change your system of labels into one that broadens your understanding.

- And, most important, challenge yourself to look beyond your own labeling process.

I know you will find that you are so much more than you originally believed when you categorized yourself according to what you thought were your appropriate labels. When I die, I want to be thought of as Tom Sullivan: husband, father, singer, actor, athlete, author, humanitarian, community activist, and, most important, friend, who, by the way, happened to be blind. My life prayer is that with God's help I can step beyond my most obvious label and extend to you my most important inner and better self. I am Tom Sullivan, flawed and imperfect, a man who often does not live up to his own expectations. But I believe in the very fiber of my soul that I, like you, have a lot to offer everyone I meet.

Face Your Fear Factor

Courage is resistance to fear, mastery of fear—
not absence of fear.
—Anonymous

Where Does Your Fear
Come From?

On the current NBC show *Fear Factor,* contestants are asked to face their fears and phobias, overcoming them and being rewarded with a large amount of cash. We see the contestants eat worms or be surrounded by snakes, or maybe leap off prodigious heights into air bags, or even hold their breath underwater upside down in a tank for an extended period of time. Although some of the participants may actually have fears that relate specifically to the challenges put before them, I believe most of what they're asked to do relates more directly to their repulsion rather than fear.

Our fears are much more deep-seated and manifest themselves in all kinds of dynamics that complicate our lives. We are all afraid of something. We must acknowledge that we are profoundly affected by our own individual fear factors. Not only is it okay to be afraid, it's a staple of what most of us would acknowledge as normal behavior. We often behave largely out of fear. It's important to analyze the content of our fears.

The first kind of fear that haunts all of us is that of the unknown. Throughout history, humans have strived to create reasons for things they cannot understand. Things happened because it was the will of the gods, or because we deemed ourselves unworthy of reward. Natural disasters had to have a reason in order for us to cope with the loss of life or property, so we defined them as acts brought about by our failure to please our deities.

Through knowledge and training, we are able to overcome our fear of the unknown and arrive at a place where we can handle our natural predisposition to be afraid. As I have mentioned, when I began to compete as a wrestler, I developed a horrible fear that my opponent was a monster. I woke up in the middle of the night soaked with sweat after having a dream that the monster had overwhelmed me by wrapping me up.

In my dreams, my opponent had at least six arms and a multitude of legs. He also made growling and snarling sounds, all designed to frighten me. I was amazed when I found out that he was a kid just like me, and that I could overcome my fear by winning matches through skill, knowledge, and hard work.

It's so easy to be limited by the fears we build up based on legend or hearsay or our own insecurity. Gaining a knowledge base is the quickest way to overcome fear of the unknown. Fear promotes anxiety, and that can be manifested by our own expectations or anticipation of a fearful event. When we anticipate a result based on fear rather than reality, or when we expect a result and don't get it, we are unable to respond with a continuing effort to achieve our goals.

Go for It!

I have often been asked to give speeches to corporations. Sometimes after reading the material sent by a company and meeting some of the top executives, I would say to Patty, "Well, I guess I'm in for a tough day today, dear. Everything points to a dead audience. They just seem like such stiff people." I've learned to approach each speech with a disciplined professionalism, always trying to do my best, so it comes as a wonderful surprise to me when I find a group of people who laugh at the right times, get emotionally involved, seem to get a great deal out of my content, and stand up at the end of my presentation to cheer my performance.

When we presuppose a result, we automatically set ourselves

up for failure. The concept that best applies to overcoming this aspect of the fear factor is to go for it.

Once you agree to get involved in an event, an activity, or a cause, don't hold back Bring your best, take a chance, let it all hang out, and go for it!

If your anticipated fear is real, you are even more equipped to cope with the results because you know you gave it your best effort. Then there's the other extreme, brought on by performance anxiety and the fear of expectation. I came to understand this when I played in the U.S. Blind Golf championships. I had diligently prepared for the event and had built up expectations of achieving success. My drives were flying high and straight. There was magic in my putter. I was sure that when I played with my friends in Florida I would acquit myself with honor.

The truth was, I believed that maybe I could win the tournament. And when we began to play, it seemed possible. At the end of the first day, I was just a few shots out of the lead and I was excited. My fear was being suppressed by my expectation—a recipe for disaster.

I had read all kinds of books and articles on how the great players prepared for the final round in a major championship. Sam Snead's approach was to stay loose by going out and partying all night. Ben Hogan locked himself in his room and wouldn't speak to anyone. I decided to strike a happy medium. I stayed in my hotel, watched a movie, and ordered a cheeseburger, a salad, and a cold beer.

The next morning, I got up early and worked out in the health club, figuring that I could reduce the stress. Then I went to the golf course and adopted a Hoganesque approach: I didn't talk to anyone with the exception of my coach. I warmed up carefully, hitting every shot with as much precision as I had ever achieved. Everything seemed on the right track, so as I walked to the first tee I expected to play very competitive golf.

That image ended three swings later. On the first tee, I hit three balls so far left that they went out of bounds, and because my expectations had been set so high, the fear factor once again raised its ugly head and I was unable to cope with my golf game for the rest of the day. I shot one of the highest rounds ever recorded in blind golf. But I learned a lot.

Bobby Jones always said, "Play it as it lies," meaning take what the game gives you and make the most out of it. By living that golf mantra, he believed that the game would come much more easily. He maintained an even keel by neither anticipating failure nor expecting results. His fear was always grounded. He appreciated the challenge of competition and understood the hard work he had put in to become a champion. From this place he accepted the highs and lows that the game imposes on even the greatest players.

The balance is achieved when we are able to blend our self-confidence with a healthy fear factor that allows us to release the adrenaline that drives us to our best results. Without understanding fear and coming to terms with all of its nuances, we can, and do, become paralyzed in its grip of indecision and self-doubt.

Redeeming Myself on National TV

It had all happened too fast. I went to work for *Good Morning, America* in the fall of 1978. One of the producers suggested to the network that I might be a perfect person to work as a substitute host when David Hartman was on vacation or assignment.

Here I was, in my early thirties, with no hosting experience, and with only a minimum of rehearsal, I was going to be on live morning television—with no possibilities of retakes or do-overs. Intro copy and questions on the interviews of the day were fed to me through an IFB earphone, with someone in the control room reading the copy so that I could say it as I heard it.

At that time, with limited technology, I was not only hearing the person reading to me but also all of the director's conversations with the cameraman as he called the shot list. It was a garbled verbal mess for a young television host to sort through. I became paralyzed by my fear of failure.

We rehearsed on Friday morning following the airing of that day's show, and I don't think I slept at all through the course of the weekend. I was completely frightened by the foreboding of what I viewed as my own imminent television disaster.

I should have faced my fear, asked for more rehearsal, and told the producer that maybe I wasn't ready for this job. But youth is often served by arrogance, and somehow I figured I would be able to bluff my way through; or maybe I just decided there was no way out of the dilemma that was causing my stomach to knot up in a ball of anxiety and fear.

At that time, Sandy Hill was David Hartman's cohost. There has never been a more enthusiastic human being in broadcasting. Sandy is smart, gutsy, and fun, and she did everything possible to make me feel comfortable on that first morning. Even with Sandy's help and support, I simply couldn't get out of my own way when dealing with my fear. In preparing to write these pages, I went back and studied the broadcast tape of my first day of hosting.

Wow. I stuttered and stammered, reversed introducing John Coleman with the weather and Kathleen Sullivan with the news, forgot to promo Rona Barrett and her "Hollywood Beat," and never asked Bill Cosby an appropriate interview question. *Good Morning, America* was number one in the morning ratings in 1979, but following my performance on that first day, the gap in the Nielsens between us and *The Today Show* probably narrowed—at least temporarily!

Later that afternoon, there was a production meeting to review the morning's show. Although people tried their best to put a positive face on my debut as a guest host I knew that colleagues were trying not to hurt my feelings.

As has been the case throughout our relationship, it was my wife, Patty, who had the courage to face the problem directly. "Look, Tom," she said, "you just weren't being yourself. You came off either as a bumbler or a news stiff. There was no relaxed Tom Sullivan in your delivery. You seemed paralyzed by your fear, like a deer in the headlights."

My wife really nailed the truth. Fear had made it impossible for me to trust my basic instincts and deliver the real Tom Sullivan to the job of hosting *Good Morning, America*. I slept better that night, understanding that all I could be was the best Tom Sullivan possible.

If you become hung up on your fear and paralyzed by your doubts or overriding concerns, you will never succeed in the workplace. If you're worried so much about your boss's opinion that you don't function effectively, you will not achieve. Shakespeare wrote, "Conscience doth make cowards of us all": it is impossible to do the right thing if we are paralyzed by our fears.

I returned to *Good Morning, America* the next day with a chance to redeem myself. The show couldn't have gone better. Even the head of daytime television at ABC invited me to lunch to express how delighted the network was with my effort.

Growing Up

There are myriad examples we can point to when analyzing the effects that fear of failure imposes on all of us. Just consider the way we educate our children. Rather than developing their strengths, we drive them to rote learning, believing that drills build skills. The true-or-false and multiple-choice concept in testing creates an either/or feeling inside a child. Consequently, the student develops fear of failure.

In corporate life, we tell our sales forces that they must sell a certain quota of product. By placing a number on their perform-ance, we force them to rush and reduce the quality of customer care. If you're an athlete, *how* you play the game is not as important as the theory of "just win, baby," because winning's the only thing that counts.

Our fear of failure can overwhelm belief in our success.

If we celebrate our successes with the same emotional intensity as our experience of fear, we develop a far richer and more positive approach to enjoying every facet of our lives.

Our minds can conjure up all kinds of things to be afraid of. When I was a boy trying to make my way in the neighborhood, facing my fear played a major role in allowing me to find my place as an equal member in the community of children. Nearby where I lived there was a lighthouse that was built in the early 1800s. It was said that this building was haunted by the old lighthouse keeper who had been murdered by the crew of a ship run aground off the Scituate coast.

It seems that the lighthouse keeper had not remembered to turn on the light that would guide the ship into Scituate harbor through the thick night fog. The investigation proved that the keeper had been drunk, and the crew took its own revenge by murdering him and throwing him off the top of the lighthouse.

Since then, the townsfolk have believed that his ghost has for-ever prowled the old building, hoping to assuage his guilt by once again turning on the light. At a sleepover party when we shared that story, we started to dare each other to find out if anybody had the guts to spend the night in this spooky house. I decided that this adventure would be perfect for me. Why should I be afraid of ghosts, I thought—I can't even see them. And so I took up the chal-lenge to spend the night alone in the old haunted house. All night, every groan, every creak, every squeak in the building was fright-ening. Was it rats, the wind, or the old lighthouse keeper? I wasn't sure, but somehow I summoned up my courage, stayed for the night, and in the morning gained the utter and total respect of the neighborhood boys.

Your honest evaluation of potential is critical if you are going to overcome all types of fear factors. For years, I struggled to ski a certain run on my beloved Winter Park Mountain. Because I was always falling and spending more time in the snow than on skis, I built up the idea that every time I tried, I would fail. It was my son, Tom, who got tough with me one afternoon and reminded me that I had skied bumps far more difficult than the ones found on the run called Gandydancer.

"Dad, you're a wuss. You're sitting back on your skis and you're not going for it because you figure you're going to fail." He was right. I skied the run perfectly, flying over the bumps as if they weren't even there.

Our fears can be overcome if we convert them to realities we understand. There are many things in life to be afraid of, but often fear is a liar, prompting us to avoid the understanding necessary to gain the higher ground of truth. Although I still carry an ongoing fear of personal failure, I believe that it's now become a healthy driving force in my psychological makeup, prompting me to try harder in my efforts to fulfill my hopes, goals, and dreams.

Seeing Lessons Reflections and Exercises

Your fears are the most significant barrier blocking the fulfillment of your hopes, dreams, and goals. You can bring the actualization of your potential to a complete halt if you allow your fears to overwhelm your efforts to gain happiness and success.

Granted, fear is a powerful force, and I do not want to suggest that overcoming your fears is easy and that the process doesn't require continuous effort and practice. You need your fear of failure to raise your level of commitment and intensity. For example, if a runner stood on the starting line waiting for the gun to go off, believing that he or she could not be beaten in the 400 meters, the adrenaline wouldn't flow, and the chances would be excellent that another athlete competing with the right mindset would go on to win the race.

Anxiety can be a healthy motivator, but for the most part fear acts on all of us with paralyzing effect. So how do you overcome your fears and actualize your true talent to achieve your goals? First, do not hide from your fears. It is critical that you recognize the significance of the things you are afraid of and not try to bluff your way through. Acknowledging your fears and phobias is the first step in coping with them. Then you must gain the best grasp possible on how important the fear factor is in a particular effort you are about to undertake. For example:

- A corporate CEO works to assess the complete business climate before making a major investment in R&D or new product development.

- A mother worried about the success of her child in school searches out the appropriate tutors who will make it possible for her child to do better.

- Athletes examine the track records of their opponents and compare those statistics to their own.

What is your situation? Evaluate it and work with it. Effective evaluation of your fear factors leads to the recognition of the steps necessary to overcome your inner demons.

Within this context, you must learn to measure the *consequence* of fear. In most cases, what you're afraid of does not constitute the end of your hopes and dreams. Fear usually connects to a specific event, a moment in time, not the collective quotient of your life. When you can segment fear to a specific moment, you compartmentalize it and can control it in most cases.

Then there's the fear developed through your establishment of false positives. This is different from bravado, because it relates to your application of false or inappropriate expectation for your own success. It is best seen when companies project sales figures that they know cannot be achieved. They do this so that employees are forced to reach for higher goals, and often the companies know the goals are impossible. They don't consider the impact that this kind of manipulation can have on the workforce.

Conditioning yourself according to your fears is as bad for your psyche as anticipating the failure found in your future concerns. If you are fearful rather than courageous, the result is an absolute certainty: you will fail. The only person who pays the price when accepting fear as a dominant part of life is you. But if you proceed in life's process with courage, you will be admired, and there will always be a helping hand ready to assist you in the achievement of any goals you choose.

Recognizing your fears, understanding your fears, overcoming your fears by fueling them with the need you have to succeed, analyzing your fears, taking risks in order to control your fears, and respecting the need to be fearful are all important if you are going to turn your fear factors into useful life positives.

Challenge Is the Pathway to Opportunity

Welcome every problem as an opportunity. Each moment is the great challenge, the best thing that ever happened to you. The more difficult the problem, the greater the challenge in working it out.

—GRACE SPEARE

Losing in Order to Gain

I'm often amazed at the significance that a seemingly minor incident can play in our lives. A comment from a friend can radically alter our behavior without the other person even being aware of the impact that his or her statement may have on our future. That's exactly what happened to me five years ago. I was fifty years old and my star quotient was at an all-time low.

There wasn't much in the way of talk television around for me. TV series were not featuring people with disabilities. As for my musical career, I was not a techno-pop writer and ballads were not the current thing. After a disappointing performance by one of my books, *Special Parents, Special Child*, I wasn't inclined toward writing another one right away.

So there I was experiencing what could only be described as fifties funk. I seemed to have lost the magic, the zing, the pizzazz, or whatever allows a creative person to get the oomph back in a stalled career.

I was with Patty shopping (something I hate to do) because there was nothing else to do. Standing at the checkout counter of the grocery store, I felt a tug on my arm.

"Hi," I said. "I'm Tom Sullivan. What's your name?"

"Eric," the young boy answered. "Weren't you on *Mork and Mindy*?"

Uh huh, I thought. The power of reruns. "Yes," I said. "Did you like the show?"

"Oh, yeah," Eric said. "Robin Williams is awesome."

I believed the next part of our conversation would be the traditional question, "May I have your autograph, please?" But that request didn't come. Instead, my four-foot-tall fan innocently asked, "So didn't you used to be famous, Mister?"

I was rocked and sort of stammered, "Oh, I guess just a little bit." Without another comment, the kid moved on with his life, and I was forced to reevaluate mine.

It's said that timing is everything, but our response to timing or moments of transition is not always appropriate. In the same week that I encountered the boy, my lawyer and close friend, John Woodward, was on the phone with me hyping one of his favorite subjects: the benefits and glory of living in the mile-high city of Denver, Colorado. I already served on the board of directors of three organizations that I treasured all located in Colorado: the National Sports Center for the Disabled, the Morris Animal Foundation, and Up With People. I thought about selling our beautiful home on the Palos Verdes peninsula and getting a fresh start out of show business in Colorado.

All the signs seemed to make sense. Our daughter, Blythe, was already working in Denver for Up With People. Our son, Tom, had decided to join that group as a performer. So why not? Let's pack up and move to the Rockies!

I also rationalized that it would be easier for me to continue my lecture career traveling from the middle of the country rather than always having to fly coast-to-coast. All the indicators pointed to a wonderful new start in the pristine beauty of Denver. And so with the real estate market in California at an all-time low, we sold our beautiful home. Why didn't we rent it? Why didn't we try Colorado for a year to see how it would work out, knowing we could return to southern California? We can get hung up on the whys of our lives, but it's important to understand that we're imperfect in our decision making.

Okay, so we moved, and Patty and I threw our best selves in to becoming real Coloradans. We bought a house in an upscale community in Englewood, a Denver suburb. It sat on the tenth hole of a Pete Dye golf course, less than a quarter of a mile from the beautiful Highline Canal, a perfect place for jogging, walking, and biking. Through my friend, John Woodward, I became an active booster of the Denver Broncos pro football team, spending a lot of time with players and another friend, Coach Mike Shanahan. I began to even consider a run for Congress or the Senate and courted Colorado Republicans concerning my prospects. Patty was active in all kinds of nonprofit community efforts. We were a couple on the move, members of the A-list, the new guys in town.

But something was wrong. Initially it was just a feeling that grew into a real awareness. Our lives were not as they seemed. We weren't happy. Why not? Because we had given up the fight too early. I had not embraced a new life in Colorado; I had quit show business. Quitting is not accepting challenge, and without the acceptance of challenge, opportunity will not knock.

The Beatles titled one of their songs "The Long and Winding Road," and that's what the path of challenge would look like if we drew it on a map. It is not a straight line. It bends and turns, sometimes even back on itself. But it inevitably arrives at its destination—*opportunity*—if our effort remains consistent and our confidence doesn't waiver.

Accepting challenge does not necessarily mean that victory will be the prize. Often we grow through our failures, which was clearly the case in my effort to become a novelist. I spent sixteen months trying to write a thriller, only to find that my talent was lacking. You can't be good at everything, and I certainly possessed only a modicum of creative aptitude when it came to being a novelist. However, in my efforts, I became a disciplined writer, starting work promptly at 9 A.M. after having put in a couple of hours of diligent exercise, writing steadily until 2 in the afternoon, then editing and correcting the previous day's work. All in all, during our time in

Colorado when show business wasn't on the radar screen, I evolved the tools necessary to take my place as a bona fide scribe, making my living from the power of the word and the pen.

My skills expanded. I wrote articles for *Newsweek, Sports Illustrated, People,* and others, then ventured into the netherworld of screenplay writing. Paddy Chayefsky and William Goldman, I'm not. Nor do I have the comedy talent of Neil Simon or Billy Wilder. But I began to understand that I possessed a powerful sense of story and an appreciation for dialogue that comes from having lived as a blind person forced to express himself verbally. In my screenplays, characters talk and talk and talk. Thank God, some of what they say makes sense, and my agent, along with studios, have come to think that I actually have a style.

None of this emergence as a creative writer would have happened without the adversity—the challenge of failure in show business. We are all subjected to circumstances that move us in ways that we would never have expected. Living in Colorado was not part of my life plan. And yet it was the Colorado experience that made me return to Los Angeles with an energy and a fervor that now has me back in the movie business more successful than before. However, we probably would not have returned to Southern California had it not been for the fact that Tom and Blythe also transitioned back home. We woke up one morning in Colorado with both of our children telling us that they were going to create new lives back in California. That catalyst prompted us to return to Palos Verdes.

Gut Checks

Do the fates control us or do we control our fate? It is a combination of all of the variables of circumstance coupled with the acceptance of challenges as pathways to opportunities. The bottom line is that if there were no challenges, if we lived in a Garden of Eden, what motivation would we have to improve our lot in life? Challenge, even adversity, forces all of us to go through real soul searching. These are moments where the rubber meets the road, where we go through gut checks. Because that's generally where the pangs start. We're nervous at the possibility of failure when we assess our capacity to cope with new challenges.

Patty and I returned to California excited and worried. Could we rekindle my show business career? I had believed that even though we had moved to Denver, opportunities in television, music, and film would keep coming my way. But the truth is, in a business based on the flavor-of-the-month, if you're out of sight, you're out of mind. I wasn't a has-been, but I certainly was a performer who had been relegated to reruns.

When Patty and I returned to California, I failed big time. I mean really big time. I couldn't find an agent. I couldn't sell a project. I couldn't get a job as an actor. We couldn't find a house. The muse had abandoned my writing, but was I a failure? Absolutely, unequivocally, definitely not. Because I still possessed the courage necessary to risk in order to gain reward.

In order to turn challenge into opportunity, three things have to occur:

1. You must see it and believe it. Sometimes your challenges aren't clear. You know you're not getting to the place you intended, but you're not sure why. If you can't see your challenges clearly, you cannot assess what it's going to take to achieve your goals. Seeing is believing.

2. You have to overcome the risk/reward syndrome. And I believe there's a parallel concept that goes hand in hand with risk/reward. Generally, the greater the risk, the greater the reward. I'm sure that each of you has a different risk

quotient. Some of you put it on the line more than others, and there isn't a formula that governs the level of risk you are willing to take.

3. You have to define your willingness to accept challenge that leads to opportunity and brings in the element of courage. Your fear of failure cripples your capacity to enjoy the sunlight of success. But what are you really afraid of when you choose not to take on challenge? And can you develop the courage necessary to risk in order to gain reward? Failure is a relative term. All of us fail. And if you evaluate your life, you would probably be surprised to realize how much more often you fail than succeed. The issue is not whether you fail—that's a given; the thing you have to figure out is whether you are going to be crippled by your fear of failure. I believe this limitation can be overcome when you recognize that you grow as much by learning from your failures as you do when you achieve your successes. Failure is a wonderful teacher. When you realize that every human being fails, the mystique surrounding the idea that failure has to be a disaster begins to lift from your shoulders.

Opportunities of the Spirit

It was early on a Sunday morning, and I had been asked to perform as well as give a testimony on the *Hour of Power* television show hosted by the Reverend Dr. Robert Schuller. I had become familiar with Dr. Schuller first through his television ministry, then because his daughter, Carol, and I both learned to ski in the National Sports Center for the Disabled in Winterpark, Colorado. Carol Schuller had lost her leg in an accident and had gone on to become one of the country's best amputee skiers. Right away, I felt connected to this man of faith. His capacity to articulate concepts that make sense in everyday life is remarkable.

On this Sunday I sang "His Eye's on the Sparrow," and Dr. Schuller spoke about dreams. He said that if you could conceive it and if you believed it, you could achieve it. I bought into this idea wholeheartedly. It is in the conception part of the dream that we must evaluate challenges, believing that we can overcome them, achieving our goals, and providing a continuum of opportunity.

Life is a continuum of opportunity.

This idea has dominated my thinking since Patty and I returned to Southern California and I met Dr. Robert Schuller.

Over the last three years, I've been able to create an entirely new career behind the camera rather than in front of it. The recognition that I was not a novelist turned my attention to writing a motivational book. The time I had spent studying screenwriting and formulating stories has led to the sale of a number of movie projects. I've become involved in three new businesses that I would not have ever discovered living in Colorado. But most important, I now have the attitude that embraces challenge as a catalyst. My career is back on the fast track and my confidence is completely renewed.

Recently, I had the wonderful experience of working as a guest star on television's *Touched by an Angel*. Roma Downey, the remarkable, beautiful Irish actress, stars with the talented and imposing Della Reese as angels sent down to earth to aid people in their pursuit of an appropriate life path based on a combination of hope and faith. These two women were a joy to work with. Week after week, Martha Williams, the creator of the show, along with her staff, turns out important scripts with life lessons all of us should be taking to heart. In my show business initiative, I had created a videotape explaining to Martha why she ought to put me on the show. Pretty gutsy, huh? Thank goodness Martha bought into the idea that maybe she could use my talent and created an episode with a wonderful part for me.

It had been four years since I had been in front of the cameras, and I didn't have my chops together. I had done at least fifty similar episodic dramas. I had taken acting classes. There was a time when I was very comfortable, even cocky, in my approach to my roles. During the years that I performed on a soap opera, I would learn fifteen or twenty pages of dialogue a day as if it were falling off a log.

Now there I was having talked my way into an episode of *Touched by an Angel* and the fear factor had raised its ugly head. I was worried that I wouldn't be any good. I was worried that they would never want me back. I was worried that it had been too long since I had acted. In short, my fear of failure was dominating my ability to accept challenge and allow opportunity to take its rightful place. During the runthrough of my first scene, a conversation with angel Roma Downey, I went up on every line. ("Going up" is what an actor does when he can't remember what he's supposed to say.) I had the script down cold on my way to the set that morning. When they were putting my makeup on, I practiced saying my lines rapidly and could spout them off like a tobacco auctioneer with rapid-fire speech. But now with the lights and cameras in place, I was a stiff. My fear of being lousy was overwhelming my capacity to be good. I could sense Roma and the crew thinking, Oh, brother, it's going to be a long week. Martha hired a lame one, and we're stuck with him.

While the cameras were being reset, Patty mercifully took me to my trailer. I was surprised at her seemingly unsympathetic approach. "Listen," she said, "you can play this part in your sleep. What's the matter with you? You're embarrassing yourself out there."

Her stinging but well-thought-out rebuke reminded me that life requires all of us to have a certain sense of competitive intensity in the way we take on challenge. As a child, I carried competitive anger into everything I did. As an adult, I've come to believe that *intensity* is a better word. There are a lot of factors that go into the acceptance of challenge, and in the end it doesn't really matter what motivation causes us to react positively. What counts is the acceptance that none of our dreams will be fulfilled unless we accept challenge as a necessary part of our evolution. I went back to the set imbued with a commitment to accept the challenge of my role on *Touched by an Angel* and never missed a line for the rest of the week. I'm no Jimmy Stewart (my favorite actor), but I'm comfortable that my performance was more than acceptable and that the folks at the show were not unhappy that I had guest starred.

Seeing Lessons Reflections and Exercises

When you do not challenge as a pathway to opportunity, you only hurt your own potential for growth. In fact, it is only through challenge that life opportunities open, pathways are made clear, and personal fulfillment becomes possible.

You may become paralyzed when the fear of failure overwhelms your willingness to accept challenge. Knowing all of this, even believing in the concept that challenge is the pathway to opportunity means nothing if steps aren't effectively taken to actualize the process through a disciplined level of personal commitment.

First, you must conceive it, see it, and believe it. the recognition of challenge begins with gaining a full grasp on what the challenge implies: the potential cost to your psychological makeup, the recognition that much will be asked of you if you are to achieve your goals, and the full knowledge that generally, success will take time and patience.

Being blind, I find it ironic that I've always been able to literally see the finish line, drawing clear pictures of how it will feel to overcome the challenge confronting me. This is the picture you have to have when beginning the quest. Without a clear picture of accomplishment, you will be weighed down by the process.

Then you come to the most complicated question facing you in the acceptance of challenge as a pathway to opportunity: Do you believe it in your heart, in your soul, and in your gut? Do you really believe in your capacity to triumph? A shaky belief system means that under the stress of adversity it is quite likely that you will fail. You must be absolute in your commitment to the idea that if you conceive it and see it, you must commit your entire heart, mind, body, and soul to believing it.

Doubt is the enemy. Despair takes up too much time. Depression is based on yesterday's news, not today's events. Fear of failure can easily overwhelm success, causing you to become paralyzed in the strenuous climb to the top of life's mountain. You may be caught on a precipice, unable to climb up and unwilling to look down. When success and failure hang in the balance, you have to develop a go-for-it attitude in your commitment to reach your goals.

But let me lighten the load when you think about challenge. A critical component in the acceptance of challenge as a pathway to opportunity has to do with whether you are willing to have fun. Challenge is fun. Competing is fun. Reaching beyond your grasp is fun. There is joy in the wondrous feeling of being completely alive when you take on the exciting experience of the challenge.

Rather than always categorizing challenge as a set of serious and weighted circumstances, why not embrace the concept with joy and enthusiasm? You've often heard people say that their work can become their pleasure. My friend Jack Nicklaus told me that golf was not only his job but his hobby. The joy he experienced in playing the game well far outweighed the challenge of competing on the most difficult courses in the world against the best players.

But what about the challenges that are imposed on you, those moments in life that test the very fiber of your soul and the basic makeup of your character? How can you cope with them?

You must remember that living is always a learning curve and challenge under fire is your greatest teacher. At fifty-five years old, I'm convinced that my blindness has provided me with the greatest opportunity to develop the insight evolved from inner vision.

The ultimate challenge of living without the capacity to see has forced me to learn all of the life lessons I'm sharing with you in this book. When I have talked to friends coping with disabilities far more complex than my blindness, I have universally found that well-adjusted people feel exactly the same way as I do.

The devastation of forest fire is necessary in order to promote nature's regrowth. Loss of life and property creates rebirth. I believe evolution is on a constant upward mobility track. We are getting better at almost everything. Physically, humans have evolved as a more healthy species. Mentally, we possess the capacity to gain more information through the development of expanded access to knowledge than ever before. We are in a new age of enlightenment. A global renaissance of art and culture is going on as people from all parts of the planet express themselves to the world.

Yes, there are conflicts raging around the globe, but I believe that most members of the community of nations seem far more committed to maintaining peaceful coexistence and an effective world order. All of this growth in who we are has come first from the willingness of each of us to accept challenge, then from understanding that only through adversity can we become complete as human beings.

I want to be presented with challenges every day. Without them, life would have no meaning, and I would probably be bored with my own existence. I'm convinced that you feel the same way. So, as my son likes to say, "Bring it on, dude." Let's start tomorrow excited at the opportunities presented by a challenge embraced, then met head on.

LIFE SECRET #12

Take a Leap of Faith

*That's one small step for man,
one giant leap for mankind.*
—NEIL ARMSTRONG

Bungee Jumping into Life

Five . . . four . . . three . . . two . . . one. Was it a countdown to death, or the most amazing, exhilarating, positive experience of my life? Was I doing this having weighed and measured every element of the decision, or was it simply whimsy? Was this a flight of fancy, a capricious whim of the human spirit, or just something stupid?

I was standing on the top of Skipper's Canyon Bridge, just outside Queenstown on New Zealand's beautiful South Island. The bridge felt wonderfully firm under my feet, but when the countdown reached zero, I was going to leap into space from a height of over three hundred feet, attached to a bungee cord secured only around my ankles. Had I gone mad? Had the stars aligned in a way that had juggled the normal thought process of my brain? Was this the onset of early senility? Did I have a death wish?

Patty and I had come to New Zealand to experience an adventure called the Awesome Foursome. It begins with a harrowing helicopter ride through narrow rock-lined canyons—not something I'd recommend for the faint of heart. Actually, as the whirlybird twisted and turned, causing all of us grave stomach distress, I was delighted not to be able to see the rock walls we rushed past within three perilous feet of the propeller blades.

Upon landing, we began the second part of our saga: a gut-churning rafting trip down a river with rapids as difficult as anything I'd experienced on the Colorado. After that, we took a nerve-wracking ride in speedboats designed to skim over water less than two feet deep, bringing us to a heart-pounding stop just under Skipper's Canyon Bridge.

So by the time we arrived at the bungee jump, adrenaline was pumping nervous energy through my entire system. Our host was one of the great characters of New Zealand sports: five-time Olympian Rod Dixon. Dixon is the only athlete in history to have run in almost all of the distance events. At one time or another, he has been a top five contender in the 1,500-, 1,800-, 3,000-, 5,000-, and 10,000-meter events, as well as the winner of the New York Marathon in world record time.

Rod is seemingly fearless, believing he is bulletproof to bodily injury. He also loves a good time, so the night before my leap, he and I shared a conversation over cold Foster's beers and oysters about our imminent folly. Looking back, I can't tell whether we were buoying up each other's spirits or playing the ego-driven game of chicken, daring each other to go through with the highest bungee jump in the world.

Regressing to my wrestling days, I turned the bungee jump into a bottomless chasm of death. After about the fourth beer, I was even thinking about who I wanted to participate in the grand eulogy that would accompany my funeral back in the States.

Sure that both Rod and I had gone around the bend, Patty did everything to talk us out of the jump. But we were men, not cowards. And the TV cameras were going to be there, so how would we back out now?

So there we were, sitting on two bar stools, talking ourselves into believing that we weren't afraid. New Zealand, particularly South Island, is probably the most beautiful place I've ever been. One day during my trip, I took a morning swim in the warm, clear water of the Pacific, took a tram to the top of a local mountain and skied during the early afternoon, and ended the day with nine holes of golf that we got in just before dark.

The only negative in New Zealand is the cuisine: It is boring. Most everything is fried and there is this stuff called Vegemite, which is probably made from something I don't want to know about.

No worries though, mate, because the people are some of the nicest a bloke could ever meet. From the prime minister to the guy pumping your gas, New Zealanders have a no-worries attitude that makes you feel comfortable in every setting—except maybe when you're standing about three hundred feet above the water on Skipper's Canyon Bridge and the guy attaching the bungee cord to your ankles says, "Right—the only time we lost someone was when we forgot to attach the bungee. Ha! Ha!"

Preparing to bungee jump must be a lot like what someone on Death Row experiences when he gets the chair: the towel around your ankles (to save on rope burns), the clamps (to secure the bungee), the request to take out your contacts, if you have any, and placing your feet at the edge of the bridge. The difference is that you take the leap of your own volition.

It is a true leap of faith. You must believe that these guys know exactly what they're doing. They tell you that thousands of people have jumped from the precipice. They even show you videos of all the different ways you can do it: head first, feet first, frontward, backward, in a chair, going double—all of these prodigious feats are possible if you just believe that they know what they're doing.

When we take a leap of faith, we are risking in order to gain reward. The balancing act is in our ability to evaluate risk and reward. The equation is different for everyone, since we all evaluate our circumstances from a unique place. For example, I am a high-risk, high-reward guy. I guess it's because I believe that in order to be equal, I always have had to do just a little more.

So I was at the top of Skipper's Canyon Bridge, listening to the countdown, my brain telling me that this was ridiculous, my stomach rebounding with the same bounce I had just been told I would get from the bungee cord.

Five . . . four . . . three . . . two . . . one . . . GO! I leaped into space, only realizing later when I watched my own video how loudly I had screamed. Does your life pass before your eyes in a moment like this? Well, in my case that didn't happen, but in the four or five seconds of freefall I had time to think about Patty and my children, to apologize to my mother for reading about my demise in her local paper, and to wonder if the insurance premium had been paid. The great part of bungee jumping is the payoff you get when you reach the bottom, as the cord snaps you all the way back to the top so that you get a second ride you feel better about because you know you're safe.

All in all, my leap of faith was a complete rush of pleasure that I wouldn't trade for anything. Would I do it again? You have to be kidding me. There is no way no how that I am ever returning to Skipper's Canyon Bridge. But the memory was worth it.

Winning occurs when inspiration blends with preparation and perspiration, allowing you to achieve your personal goals. You must be inspired in order to take a chance, to go for the gold. Obviously, you must also prepare, examining all the possibilities that will either enhance or detract from your success.

And then you must perspire. It's necessary to do the work and be willing to pay the price required to gain the reward.

Faith is the abracadabra part—the magic of it all, the element of confidence that causes miracles to occur, the belief that makes hope live in our hearts and inspire our souls. It is also the essential connector for interaction. A couple believes in fidelity to make their marriage work. A child believes that her parents are right when they encourage her to take a chance and pursue a dream. As members of a free society, we try to have faith that our leaders are making decisions to serve our best interests. We get on an airplane, entrusting our safety to a pilot. We believe our doctor is prescribing the right medicine, and trust that our religious and spiritual pastors can guide us on a path of righteousness. We must keep the faith.

Keep the Faith on Life's Stage

Twenty-five years ago, I said that to former Miss America Mary Anne Mobley seconds before we performed a high-flying trapeze act in television's *Circus of the Stars.* I was in my mid-twenties, and to paraphrase an old chestnut, baby needs shoes. Patty and I were flat broke. My record career hadn't yet gotten underway, and I was just beginning to be known on television. So when the opportunity to make $25,000 presented itself, hey, I wouldn't have cared what was involved short of committing a crime.

Circus of the Stars was an effort by CBS to have celebrities perform stunts on a prime-time special. In my year, Mary Anne's husband, Gary Collins, walked the high wire; Richard Roundtree from *Shaft* jumped from 100 feet into the Ring of Fire; Betty White, television's Golden Girl, worked in an elephant act; and Jamie Lee Curtis performed a trapeze act. We even had performers putting it on the line with lions and Bengal tigers. Were we all crazy or greedy?

In my case, what began as simply a for-profit undertaking changed when I met stunt coordinator Bob Yerkes. Bob had been working in movies for twenty-five years, performing some of the most amazing stunts in Hollywood history. He also had come from a long line of circus flyers and was the most diligent teacher and coach with whom I ever worked. Safety was his watchword, and he did not treat us with kid gloves. We prepared our act for five months, and there was no fooling around. The only glitch was that Mary Anne and I never actually worked together until our performance. It was hard to get our schedules to coordinate and we each needed to train with a professional circus artist to learn to do our jobs.

My trainer was an amazing young woman named Beth Neufer. Beth was physically the strongest female I'd ever met. When she clamped her hands on my wrists or did an inverted angel, in which she held onto me with her legs, her power and confidence were awesome. By the time show day came along, I was sure that I had my part of the act together.

Early on in my training, Bob Yerkes had spent a lot of time making sure that I knew how to fall into the net. "Just relax," he'd tell me. "Tuck your chin into your chest, roll onto your back with your arms at your sides, and let the net absorb the fall. Don't flail or thrash, just fall."

From 85 feet above the ring, I was going to hang upside down by my feet from a still bar. Then Mary Anne would swing out into space and I would catch her and hold her while she performed various gymnastic stunts hanging from my hands without the benefit of a net. This routine was called the web, and it had been done by circus performers for years.

Lucille Ball, our mistress of ceremonies, was preparing to announce us as I was sent up the ladder to the applause of the skeptical audience. They wondered what would happen to the guy in pink tights and the star-spangled girl. The audience wasn't alone in their thoughts. Before I ascended the ladder, Lucille Ball leaned close to my ear, saying in her gruff baritone, "Kid, you've got be kidding. Let's pull the plug on this right now. You don't have to go up there."

"Yes, I do," I said, with too much vibrato. "I need the money."

So much had changed from the way we practiced. The lights had made every step of the ladder sweat from the heat they generated. When I got to the trapeze, it felt clammy. My perspective really got scary as I listened to the fading voices of the audience below.

We had another little problem. Earlier in the show, Mary Anne had performed a rope act, in which she did all kinds of spins and turns on a tightrope along with high-risk catch-and-release moves. During the act, the rope had cut into her hands, so she had to wear bandages throughout our performance. I realized that if my friend could not close her hands around my wrists, I would have to bear the full brunt of her weight. If I wasn't perfect in my execution, Mary Anne could fall.

As I dropped into position upside down above the ring, I remember thinking that I believed in my training. I had faith in Bob Yerkes. And, most important, I knew Mary Anne trusted me. Trust can be a burden, but it is the glue that holds us together and brings out our best in every life circumstance.

Our circus debut was flawless. We did not make one mistake. And as we came down the ladder to thunderous applause, Bob and Beth greeted us at the bottom with hugs and high fives. "You guys were real flyers," they told us. "You're part of the circus family. We knew you could do it. We all knew you could do it."

They knew we could do it and we knew we could do it. Our mutual commitment of faith made it possible to achieve more than either of us would have ever believed was possible when we began our training odyssey five months earlier.

To really understand the relevance of faith in your life, it's necessary to talk about the blending of belief in yourself with trust in others. I believe in myself. But blindness has made me understand that I must trust others—whether it's my life mate, Patty, or my companion guide dog, Partner; whether it's skiing with Blythe or playing golf with Tom lining up the shots.

Believing in others is as important as believing in yourself.

Certainly, when you commit yourself to believing in others, you run the risk of being disappointed. All of us can remember moments in which we felt crushed by the failure of someone else to do his or her part.

Fidelity, Faith, and Love

Your ultimate sense of well-being comes from moments when your faith is fulfilled by another person. I can remember how often I told our children that everything would be all right, then wondered if I really could deliver on what I said. The innocence of children allows them to accept without question that if you say everything will be okay, it will be. The most upsetting moments for parents are when they aren't able to fulfill their commitment. Thank goodness children accept our imperfections and go on loving us.

Fidelity goes hand in hand with faith. In a husband and wife relationship, two people work to be full of faith. The reality is that over the years passion may wane, but it's replaced by something even richer: love evolves when it is built on a foundation of faith. As marriage vows note, you will be there in sickness and in health, for richer or poorer, better or worse, till death do you part. The ability to succeed on life's journey is enhanced when you have a partner who will support your every effort unequivocally. Having faith in this idea allows you to leap into the unknown, fearful but also fearless in your knowledge that you are not alone.

You may have noted that in this chapter I have not discussed religious faith. That's because I do not believe that one person has the right to presume the beliefs of another. But I will share a thought based on life observation: People who have a faith in God and apply it to their daily process are clearly more focused in their decision making. They are ships that find their way home in a storm, believing that their faith is as constant as the northern star. Trusting in God allows people to be more at peace when coping with a life crisis that seems not to have easy answers.

I have never been particularly religious. I believe in God, but I tend to take the position that if God exists and I live a proper and effective life, I'll be granted whatever heavenly peace is provided.

We all recognize that some circumstances occur for no appropriate reason—for example, an accident in which someone is paralyzed, a heart attack at an early age, or the death of a child from cancer or some other incomprehensible illness. Those who do not have faith in a higher power may be angry at their own ineptness to understand, but people who have abiding faith seem to have abiding peace.

I do not want to send the wrong message. People of faith do in fact struggle with things they cannot understand. But if your faith is strong, you may be more able to come to terms with life elements that are unknown. You can mitigate your risk of failure through effective preparation.

Mary Anne and I trained for five months before we flew on the trapeze. The guys in New Zealand may have seemed casual, but they took extreme precautions to guarantee my safety in the bungee jump. Skiing with Blythe did not start on the toughest slopes of Colorado. I remember very clearly that we began on the bunny hill.

In the final analysis, even with effective preparation and hard work, successful human beings all risk to gain reward. All winners who I've been privileged to be around believe that success comes from a leap of faith. And you know what? Taking that leap is a hell of a ride and a lot of fun.

Seeing Lessons Reflections and Exercises

Faith is a leap. If there were a fire in your home and you were on the fourth story hanging from a ledge as men below held up nets begging you to jump, promising you that they would catch you, would you leap? You know you would, because the flames would soon be licking at your fingertips. You would jump saying a silent prayer that the people below would save you. Faith in anything—in God, in family, in friends, in self—requires you to make a choice. Do you believe? Will you take the chance? Faith is not a thermostat that you turn on and regulate, hoping to find a temperature that fits your particular personality. Faith is a light switch. You either turn it on or off. The choice is up to you.

- Strengthen your faith through hard work and preparation.

- Condition yourself to support your faith by fulfilling it through examples under fire.

- Affirm your faith every day through the consistency of your actions.

- Maintain faith if you believe it is your destiny to be success.

Developing faith through trial and error is your promise to yourself that you can believe; and when faith takes on the quotient of trust in another person, in God, or in self, it becomes active and strong. Trust becomes faith's action verb. I must believe in myself, but I also must believe in you if I'm going to achieve my goals and become the best person possible.

The paranoia of mistrust shatters your capacity to believe. I am committed to the idea that people can be trusted for the most part. I believe there is an inherent goodness in all of us that can be tapped into as we interact with each other.

Do bad things happen to good people? Without question. But do good things happen to those who openly express through faith the willingness to trust in the other? All the time. Every day, in every experience.

Faith in a higher power is a mystery, and in order to believe in that higher power, you are required to take a leap of faith.

Believing in each other is somewhat easier, because the results are measurable. Learning about others, coming to understand where they're coming from, risking with them in order to learn and grow, working to love them unconditionally (even though it is often difficult)—all of these possibilities begin with a leap of faith, then an application of trust. It is your most difficult test, but it is also your most necessary commitment if you are going to move beyond the boundaries of prejudice and bigotry. I must leap off the bridge attached by a bungee, believing that you will be there to hold me. You must be sure that as you swing out on a trapeze, I will catch you.

In these allegories and in your own life experience, you are forced to bet on me, to take a chance, to risk disappointment in order to gain the gift of friendship. You must embrace faith if you are going to connect, grow, achieve, and prosper.

Create a Life Plan

Go confidently in the direction of your dreams.
Live the life you have imagined.
—HENRY DAVID THOREAU

Chase Your Dreams

If I assessed my life in musical terms, it is clear as I enter my fifty-fifth year that I have been an improviser rather than a composer. I have let feeling and soul carry me from one thing to another, improvising the notes, interpreting based on the emotion of the moment, living my life as it comes.

My approach to the creative arts demonstrates my capricious nature. When I was chasing my dream to make records and write songs, I was also writing books, working for *Good Morning, America*, acting, starting to develop as a lecturer, participating in nonprofit foundations, raising my children, running marathons and triathlons, and basically filling every minute of my day and most of my nights with projects, all of which seemed important but crowded into a completely disorganized lifestyle.

In retrospect, I have to face the fact that much of the work suffered because I was always scrambling to catch up and pick up the pieces. I was always behind schedule, either because I was too busy doing something else or because I procrastinated, then went a little crazy trying to fulfill a deadline imposed on me either by my employer or by my own unrealistic sense of capability to complete the task.

I guess I believed that somehow I would pull it off and come out of any situation smelling like a rose. When you live like that, you ride the thin line between confidence and arrogance, and there is no question that along the way you disappoint a fair number of colleagues, family, and friends.

In my thirties, I considered it fashionable to arrive at the airport just in time to catch my flight. It was cool to put my seat belt on just as the pilot was making his final announcements before takeoff. A couple of times, I got really excited when I was able to convince the airline to turn the plane around and bring it back to the gate just to pick me up.

What was I thinking? First, my approach was selfish. Who the hell did I think I was to inconvenience everyone else's schedule? But second, why would anyone want to go through that kind of stress? Now I'm the fellow who gets to the airport with enough time to sit and read the paper, make some last-minute phone calls, have a latte, and generally chill out.

I suppose you could say I've mellowed. More than that, I just don't want the stress.

The alternative to this stress is to create a life plan.

Abundance and Your Life Plan

Recently, Patty was the chairwoman of a women's wellness conference called Simple Abundance benefiting our Little Company of Mary Community Health Foundation. It is a marvelous day designed for women and a few token men like me who get to demonstrate our strong feminine side by participating in the conference.

The speaker list has grown to be terrific, and I have been touched by many of the presenters. But it was Beth Rothenberg, a certified life coach, a business consultant, and a contributor to *Shape* magazine, who really opened my eyes to the need for all of us to develop a life plan. Beth began by reminding us that we all possess a life dream.

That was easy for me to understand. I had been a person chasing my dreams over the complete course of my professional and personal life. I had been extremely lucky, fulfilling a lot of them. I had climbed out of the darkness of my disability, found the woman who has made me happy, raised two terrific children, and made a great living. I believed I had been valuable to the world at large.

But now I realized that I was still searching to fulfill the most important dream of all. I understood that at my core I needed to leave a legacy, something that would live beyond my time on this earth to remind people that I had been here.

I realized that I would fulfill my leave-behind by working to change people's perception of what it means to be blind. On that special afternoon, I vowed that I would bring people to a different place, where they would consider disability as only one aspect of a human being. So I would be remembered as a singer, actor, athlete, author, father, humanitarian, and husband who happened to be blind—not as a blind person who did other things.

In the months following the conference, I have developed an action plan to fulfill my dream and have become affiliated with Lions International as their global ambassador. The Lions Clubs have been the most important source for funding programs for the blind around the world. Four million dedicated members have given away hundreds of millions of dollars to worthwhile projects, and now I have the chance to add to the legacy begun when Helen Keller called on the Lions to become her knights of the blind.

What Do You Want?

When it's all said and done, and you've cleared away the baggage and gotten down to the nitty-gritty of honest personal evaluation, what do you really want in your life? There's no question that people who achieve their goals and gain success have two things in common:

1. They know exactly what they want.
2. They formulate a plan to get it.

We can all point to people who seem to carry a tunnel vision mentality. By executing their life plan, they have guaranteed their future. So what did I want for my future now that I was back in California? I made a list:

- We would live in our beloved Palos Verdes community.
- I would pursue a career principally in moviemaking.
- I would limit my nonprofit participation to the work I have recently taken on with Lions International and the work I continue to enjoy with the Morris Animal Foundation.
- I would raise my level of fitness.
- I would cut back on my consumption of alcohol.
- I would spend more quality time with Patty.
- I would improve my golf swing.
- I would support the career growth of our children.
- I would focus on the quality rather than the quantity of my life.
- I would pay attention to the special moments with people I love.
- I would consider public service in my sixties.
- I would be more thrifty with our financial resources.
- I would have a future with a more appropriate sense of balance and focus.

Examine what obstacles stand in the way of the things you really want. Do you need more education, for example? I believe that's a given, because all of us need to enhance our level of learning. But in order to do it, we have to make the time, pay the price, and be willing to put in the effort.

With access to the Internet, there's no excuse not to continuously expand our educational framework. We often don't want to work hard enough at new tasks that require training. Unfortunately, we may not have the family support necessary to sacrifice in order to make the future happen. The bottom line is, Do we really want it badly enough, and are we willing to work hard enough to achieve our goals?

We also tend to worry too much about what others may think. We must trust our own instincts, set our own course, allow the breeze of hope to fill our sails, send our ship skimming across the water, and move on our journey to fulfill the bright future we've planned.

Beth told us about setting goals or plateaus of different heights as we climb life's mountain of dreams. I decided that my five-year goals are:

- To have made three meaningful films
- To have achieved complete financial independence
- To be healthier at sixty than I am at fifty-five
- To own the home that Patty and I expect to reside in for the rest of our lives

For my three-year goals, I would add helping my son, Tom, facilitate his recording career, winning the World Blind Golf Championships, and taking the first steps toward public service. Then there are the one-year goals. I will complete this book, finish *Adventures in Darkness*, the movie I'm currently working on, run a marathon with my friend Clayton Cobb, expand my communication with my sisters, and focus more attention on the quality of the lectures I give to corporations.

You can break this process down further into monthly, weekly, and even daily goals. I'm learning as I make plans that I'm much less stressed.

There are some important signposts that will define whether

you are succeeding in carrying out a plan. The goals must be clear. Beth recommends that they be very specific and that you write them out and read them often to make sure that they are stated clearly. There can be no copping out when it's all there in black and white.

Every goal has to be measurable. You must have the ability to quantify exactly how you're doing, because we all make excuses for not succeeding if our accomplishments can't be measured. Beth recommends setting up a structure on a plateau or pyramid basis. There's no question that we need to place target dates of completion on our goals, but I believe that there must be some built-in flexibility, because your effort and intent really count a lot when defining the effectiveness of your life plan.

Manage Your Time

Another element in establishing a successful plan has to do with the best use of time. Learning to make proper use of time in order to carry out a life plan is paramount in determining its completion. Beth suggested that it's important to get rid of the things that weigh us down. They drain our energy, sap our enthusiasm, and cause us emotional stress.

Because I'm an affable human being, I often get placed in situations where I waste tremendous amounts of time communicating with people who are really not an important part of my life. I am determined to reduce the energy I spend on meaningless relationships and apply it more directly to providing the people I love with the best Tom Sullivan I can be. I also need to learn to say no more often and not take on more responsibility than I can handle.

Beth suggested that we pick ten things that we do for ourselves to create a feeling of well-being. I have to admit that when I examined my list, ten seemed like a pretty small number. There were at least fifty things I did that gave me a feeling of fulfillment.

Beth talked about balancing all the factors that affect personal well-being. "You can have the best plan in the world, but if you're not in balance, even if your operational approach is correct, you won't be happy. Because no plan is perfect. So if you aren't centered, you will become frustrated by all of the elements that push and pull on you from all different directions," she said.

I was reminded of my favorite thoughts on balance from Robert Fulghum. He noted: "Live a balanced life. Learn some, and think some, and draw and paint and sing, and dance every day some." Only you can know the combination that's right for you.

There is a rightness when balance is in place, and all of us understand it readily. The question is how to obtain it. How do you find the center that lets you stand firmly on life's tightrope without fear of falling? Certainly, having a life plan is a major part of the equation, but I think even more significant is your willingness to listen to your own inner voice, the instincts you have to just know.

Recently, I've been working with a personal trainer. We've found that because of my blindness, I have a very difficult time standing on one foot and establishing a center point. We've figured out it's largely because I can't place my eyes on a spot on the wall, so my brain is constantly forced to recalculate, side-to-side and backward and forward, the subtle movement of my body as it continuously compensates for the change in my weight distribution. Having a plan, following your instincts, and trusting your core allow you to keep your eyes fixed on a goal, creating life balance— exactly what I learned to do on a physical level by creating the mental image of a spot on the wall my brain could hold onto.

For each of us, balance is different, requiring different levels of rest, work, play, relaxation, sleep, calorie intake, friendship, isolation, and human interaction. We all have the capacity to find our own center—the balance point that allows us to stand firmly on one foot while our eyes are fixed on the horizon of our own hopes, goals, and dreams.

Seeing Lessons Reflections and Exercises

Since I began writing this book, I've been asking most of my friends, colleagues, and a large number of acquaintances whether they had ever created or actively followed a life plan. My highly unscientific random survey pointed out that only 5 out of every 100 people I spoke to had ever really considered creating a strategic life plan. However, when I asked them if they worked for companies that wrote strategic plans, or whether they had ever been involved in the creation of those plans, over half of the folks I spoke with answered in the affirmative. One guy even told me, "How the hell could you run a company without having a strategic plan? It would be a lot like trying to put a man on the moon without effective preparation."

Commander Gene Sarnen, one of America's most decorated astronauts, is a good friend of mine. He told me that at the beginning of NASA the entire process was, to say the least, pretty loose. He said it was held together only by guts, theory, and even a little duct tape.

We know that battles in war have often been fought without the development of effective strategy, and certainly on Sunday afternoon when we watch pro football, we know that although there is a game plan, much of the success of the teams depends on the individual effort of the players involved. Still, I'm convinced that more success is gained through the development of a well-organized life plan than through random choice.

So what makes a good strategic plan? First, begin with an effective vision statement. What is it that you hope to be, or achieve? Usually when a vision statement is created, there's a time line attached to it so that later in the plan you can apply the strategic steps necessary to carry it out. For example, a company might say, "We intend to be the leading manufacturer of X in ten years. We intend to provide the best service in the industry to deliver our product in a timely manner, and to do it in the most cost-effective way possible." The company would then write a mission statement with the methodology needed to carry out the vision. It might include the following steps:

- Assess the position of the competition vis-à-vis what we need to do to become number one in the industry.
- Determine who our clients are and how we can best penetrate the competition's market share.
- Evaluate our current workforce and determine whether our efficiency can be increased by either expanding or decreasing our employee base.
- Evaluate cost with an eye toward both reducing our own expense and passing that benefit on to the client.

A mission statement, whether it's for a corporation or an individual, can be as extensive as necessary in order to fulfill the stated goals of the vision statement. Once the vision and mission statements have been put in place, you can focus on the time line and goal setting. Consider time lines against all of the factors that may slow your plan down when a best case has been made for the plan based on all of the available information.

We all need mentors and models, and, if possible, a strategic plan should have a model from which to work. Often, there's a section in a corporate plan called Collaborative Interviews in which the company talks to people who have been there and done that. Most corporate strategic plans also contain best-case/worst-case scenarios, with built-in adjustments for time lining and goal setting. In most strategic plans, there is an attachment for cost analysis. Your individual plan should assess who else is affected by the decisions you make, and whether the consequences of your actions place an undue burden on your family, friends, and colleagues.

A brilliant friend of mine who is the CEO of a Fortune 100 company once told me that the real secret to a strategic plan is to remember that it is a living document and remains flexible, adapting to the changes brought on by the changing environment in which it lives. He was discussing corporations. Certainly we, as fallible human beings, need even more flexibility than a global conglomerate.

Allow yourself to make mistakes. Learn to cut yourself a lot of slack in the way in which you implement your plan. But also hold to the goals and the course you set so that you feel good about yourself and are satisfied with your achievements.

Review your plan periodically. Companies do this on an annual or semiannual basis, usually on weekend board retreats, often in beautiful, exotic places. I highly recommend that in the designing of your own individual strategic plan you take the time to find a great place to rest, revitalize, and evaluate where you are in the execution of your goals.

For me, this usually means Pebble Beach, where Robert Louis Stevenson wrote that he had finally seen the most beautiful confluence of land and ocean on earth. In this extraordinary place, I find that I become recharged and completely revitalized as I evaluate the progress I'm making toward the goals outlined in my plan.

The danger in the design of a strategic plan is that we can be almost paranoid about its execution. Along with providing ourselves with the slack to let the plan be a living document that we adjust, we must also be willing to say that we are remarkable creatures with an immense capacity to improvise, to see a set of circumstances arise, then demonstrate flashes of brilliance as we fly by the seat of our pants, succeeding in ways that delight and surprise us.

A strategic plan is a blueprint, an architectural rendering of what can be, but the magic, the art, the uniqueness of the project is discovered when a flexible strategic plan is implemented with our unbelievable improvisational capacity to achieve beyond our wildest dreams. Does it sound improbable or impossible? Not if you examine history, replete with remarkable examples of achievement. And does this maxim relate to all of us?

Miracles happen when ordinary people do extraordinary things, and ordinary people do extraordinary things when they implement an effective strategic plan, bearing their remarkable uniqueness.

So plan the work and work the plan, knowing that it will lead to gratification and extraordinary personal fulfillment.

Trust Your Basic Instincts

*Trust your instinct to the end, though
you can render no reason.*
—Ralph Waldo Emerson

What Is Your Basic Instinct?

All of us have experienced the impact of basic instincts, but we often don't give them the credibility we should. We've all said things like, "I just had a feeling about that person"; or, "I knew I should have handled that situation differently"; or, "If I only had followed my intuition"; or, "I just should have gone with my gut reaction." These statements relate to our recognition that we posess a level of awareness that goes beyond logic or judgment, knowledge or information.

Instinct is nonscientific and nonquantifiable, yet scientists and psychologists are always trying to come up with complex formulas to justify what is simply as basic as being alive. In medical journals, we read about our attraction to another person being governed by the release of pheromones, which are chemical indicators that create mutual sexual attraction. If that's the case, does it happen through touch or smell, taste or sound—or is it visual? Is it an invisible chemical that hangs in the air that we pick up on through some miraculous telepathic power? We don't really know what instinct is. Scientists go on to tell us that it relates to the capacity of the brain to function as the ultimate computer, correlating the data of a lifetime into instant judgments released in nanoseconds from somewhere in the cerebral cortex. Much too complicated. Much too confusing and technical.

The closest corollary I can come up with is that instinct is like a human tuning fork vibrating at a frequency that is perfectly pitched at A 440. When I was young, I learned to tune pianos, and it was always a thrill to tap the tuning fork, then match the 440 vibrations of cycles per second to the note A in the middle of the piano. When the sound waves were an exact match, the tone was in balance, in place—perfect.

That's what happens when we experience the blending of our instincts with all of the other capacities we're so blessed to be able to use. I'm finding that as I grow older, I pay more attention to what they're telling me.

Instincts are not active in the process of gathering information. They are the repository for a collection of information taken in by our senses, experience, and judgment. They are different from judgment in that they are about feeling—that intuitive ability that goes beyond any standard form of measurement.

In Life Secret #13, we discussed the formulation of a life plan: bringing structure and order to the process of living. Sometimes our instincts will work as a corollary to that plan, an affirmation of what is possible, but there will be moments when they seem to be functioning in complete juxtaposition to the logic of an organized plan.

The Instinct of Love

On June 16, 1968, I began my career in show business by playing piano and singing in a brand-new Cape Cod nightspot called Deacon's Perch, just outside Yarmouth Port in Massachusetts. I shared this gig with another Harvard student and we were having the time of our lives.

By mid-June, we had become the rising stars of the Cape Cod night scene. On weekends, the line to get into the club stretched around the block. The nightlife was incredible. Women, parties, and booze were plentiful. We would finish work at 1 A.M., party until dawn, sleep all day, get up, and start all over again. Finding a serious relationship certainly was not anywhere in my thinking, and I clearly was not applying any kind of strategic or structural plan to my free-and-easy lifestyle.

I had never experienced this kind of freedom before. In the first place, I was making money—$200 a week, which I thought was a fortune. I was living with three guys who were as crazy as I was. I had just turned twenty-one, the drinking age in Massachusetts, and I was being treated like a star in all the restaurants and bars I frequented.

When my partner told that me that the same two beautiful girls were at table 3 for the fourth night in a row, I figured conquest, score, another notch on the belt, more stories to tell my roommates. In my wildest dreams, I never expected to meet or fall in love with Patty Steffen. And even if I had, I never would have believed that less than a year later I would be standing at the front of a church as the most beautiful girl in the world came down the aisle and pledged to love, honor, and cherish me.

So what happened? What was the catalyst that turned that June evening into a shared lifetime? Instinct. Both of us knew instantly that something special was going on. We understood that the chemistry of connection was right. We laughed easily; we talked easily; and although we didn't know very much about each other, I remember going back to my house late that evening and talking my roommate's ear off about this girl who was fantastic. And in another cottage on Cape Cod, Patty kept her friends up all night talking and wondering about what it might be like to be the wife of a person who was blind.

What was amazing even on that first evening was how easily she adapted to my disability. It seemed that her instincts were to treat me as if my disability were only one part of the person she was getting to know. That concept is exactly the one I have preached and fought for all my adult life. Patty understood it instantly without having to be told. And the application of instinct went even further—in hindsight, I came to understand that it wasn't just attraction that brought us together but a mutual recognition that we were meant to be soulmates. Over the years, when times have been tough or communication has not been at its best, we've always been able to rely on our basic instinctive sense that the other was the only person either one of us was meant to love.

Instinct and Decisions

Instinct is a powerful part of the decision-making process. I can't place a measurable degree on the difference between impression and instinct, but I'm convinced you know exactly what I mean. Impressions are fallible and can be changed. Instinct is usually infallible, because it employs all of our internal and external antennae, collecting and collating impressions in the brain, a central computer, then opening the channels to the mind's evaluation center, allowing us to utilize this most important evaluation tool.

We've often heard people comment that they know someone who has bad instincts: Let's say a person who has been married four times and is out there looking for number five. Or the guy who seems to pick horrible friends who bring no benefit to his life. I don't think that our perception of bad instinct is accurate—I believe that each of us has the same basic instincts—but the applications of these instincts relates to whether we open the channels of possibility, then make a commitment that is fundamental to success.

You must trust your basic instincts, and you must clear away the roadblocks that limit your access to this most powerful life force. Bigotries, prejudices, labels, predispositions, snap judgments, and conservative choices close off your capacity to be affected by instinctive messages.

We are often afraid to go there, to let our logical minds back off and our instincts to become amplified. My life has been greatly enhanced as I have allowed my instincts to govern the decisions I make. This is not to suggest that logic, knowledge, advice, and discipline don't play a part in our evaluation process; in fact, instinct does not govern many day-to-day decisions. But we should let it find its rightful place in our personal evolution, prompting us to become the best we can be.

Seeing Lessons Reflections and Exercises

Let's take a look at the role our instincts play. Let's say, for example, we work in sales, and we call on a customer hoping to make a deal to sell our product. In my sales experience, the key to success comes when you find the other guy's button, identifying his need and instinctively recognizing the approach you can take to guarantee the sale.

Is he a nuts-and-bolts guy, meaning, "Just give me the facts, tell me about your product, let me try it, and get out of the way so that I can convince myself I want to buy it from you"? Is he a dialogue kind of person? Does he want you to enter into extended discussions on how to use the product, or what you believe might be the best applications of the product for his business needs? Maybe he's the kind of customer who doesn't really want you to talk about the product at all but is more interested in who you are, and what kind of character you demonstrate.

It is your instinct that governs the appropriate playing field of your human interaction, because essentially that's all you have to go on. Remember, you've just met this person, and you are quickly formulating impressions that allow you to be effective in your communication. Your instinct is the only real effective tool you have to frame the success or failure of your sale.

It's even more marked when you apply for a job. What does the interviewer want from you, and what is his or her predisposition? While the interviewer is checking you out, you're applying every instinct to try to read what this person is looking for in you. You must apply every one of your senses, judgments, pieces of background information, and communication skills are under the operational modality of human instinct.

You're working for that perfect pitch, when the note is tuned perfectly at 440, vibrating with the same sound wave signature as a tuning fork. Your instinct tests the waters, evaluates the mixture, reads the signs, defines the course of action, and tells you when to back off if you're wrong.

Instinct is the single most important element in your capacity to evaluate your environment, your circumstance, and other people. Your instinct:

- Commits you to believing you're in love
- Supports the investment you make in a friend and the creation of a lifetime friendship
- Tells you that a job is right or that you've found your first house
- Tells you that a person is just not the right friend for your children to hang out with

Instinct is as close as you can get to finding perfect pitch, the right note, the correct rhythm, your own individual life song; your instinct, however, can be out of tune when biased by your individual needs—for example, you can convince yourself that someone is the right person for you to love even when your instinct is telling you that he or she is not.

I believe you are never wrong when you can say you absolutely know what's right for you. When your instinct gets that far off course, there are other factors involved, and you cannot blame your instinct for your individual failures.

Here's my formula for using instinct: In any circumstance, start by allowing your instinct to speak to you free and unfettered, then go back and apply your best logic and knowledge to the decision you're going to make. If your instinct and logic agree, go for it. If not, try to buy yourself a little more time to evaluate. But in the end, trust your instinct. It might be helpful to design steps that allow you to gradually determine your final course of action. Whenever your basic instinct speaks to you strongly, trust it, trust it, trust it.

As I See It

What lies behind us and what lies before us are tiny matters compared to what lies within us.
—OLIVER WENDELL HOLMES

It's amazing how alive you can feel on a summer night, when the sun has set and the fog's rolled in. You can be completely cocooned, at peace and safe.

Recently, I sat alone in our backyard, allowing the day to run down and the night to settle over the neighborhood. As in the morning, a robin's song trilled from the big tree at the far end of the yard.

The moisture in the air allowed me to take in the smells from all directions, and sounds seemed amplified, closely held, wrapped by the ocean's fog. My big German shepherd, Partner, lay at my feet; a rare Irish whiskey was in my left hand, and I sipped it and puffed alternately on a gaudy Macenudo Cuban cigar.

It had been a perfect day. In the morning, the dog and I had enjoyed a run and swim with our friends. I had attended some successful meetings on two of my movie projects and even squeezed in nine holes of golf, thanks to Daylight Savings Time. Patty, as usual, had made a delicious dinner, so there I was rocking on the back patio, considering the nature of life as I see it.

My mind went to the old Scottish hymn, "Amazing Grace": "I once was lost, but now am found, was blind, but now I see." So what did I see? I wasn't seeing in an external visual sense but rather with the mind's eye. How does my vision of life offer you the possibility of a different perspective?

In this book, I've tried to shine an inner light that I hope is at least different, and at best, unique, from your perspective. Because life as I see it certainly comes from a different place. I embrace the complete synergism of the senses—a coming together of touch, taste, smell, and sound that is available to all of us if we are willing to invest the time in training ourselves to pay attention to all of our sensory inputs and the world that surrounds us.

I sat in the gathering darkness, and I alternated between turning the senses on in chorus and soloing them out individually, focusing on something specific in my immediate environment. Applying myself to smell, I could tell exactly what my next-door neighbor had barbecued that evening. Understanding that the wind was blowing softly on shore, the ocean's fragrance was extremely pungent, made more dynamic by the thick evening fog. Patty's roses were in bloom, accompanied by someone's freshly cut grass.

When I turned my attention to sound, there were some kids playing pick-up basketball down the street. My neighbors were cleaning up their dinner barbecue. The robin's song had been replaced by the soft cooing of a dove, and Mozart drifted on the breeze from someone's stereo across the street.

My taste buds were being overwhelmed by a wonderful blend of thirty-year-old whiskey and a rare Cuban cigar chased down with deep breaths of the ocean's fragrance.

Touch was being taken up in a more intimate way, as the big dog had rolled onto my bare feet, allowing me to keep them warm as the heat of the day ebbed from the surface of the patio.

Patty was listening to her favorite artist, James Taylor, on the stereo as she did the dinner dishes. Every once in a while, her own singing would punctuate the chorus of the song. Patty has a great musical ear, even though she believes she can't carry a tune, and I love to listen to her sing. On this night, not only was her voice drifting on the wind but so was the faint smell of her perfume.

At this moment of quiet solitude, was I sorry that I was unable to see? Not one bit. I was reveling in the joy of what I had been given rather than what had been lost.

Youth does not always serve us well, and certainly I don't want to suggest that Patty and I haven't had the very normal moments of stress common to all marriages. But the truth is that when we recognized our interdependence, we became people who held on to a rock-solid foundation of appreciation, mutual respect, and fundamental commitment.

There is no doubt that love is the strongest tie available, bonding all of us together. But it cannot withstand the onslaught of selfishness, lack of appreciation, and not recognizing the need for interdependence. In this context, I believe that it's easy to project mutual interdependence in all aspects of our human interaction and nature's order.

Sitting there on a warm California summer night, I realized that I felt pretty good about myself. My self-image had found its balance, although the road to self-worth had not been easy. The categorization that others had applied to me as a blind person, rather than a person who happened to be blind, had definitely caused anger and pain. And yet I had arrived at a place where I had come to understand that the question of our labels has to do first with how we feel about ourselves, then with developing the capacity to assess where others are coming from.

Wearing a label is not all bad; in fact, it's even necessary if we're going to carry a positive sense of self-worth into every activity and relationship that affects our lives. But we often fall into the trap of quantifying who we are based on the pigeonholing applied to us by others.

My son, Tom, walked across the patio on his way to the garage to get his car and head out for the evening. "Hey, Dad," he said over his shoulder, "don't forget we're playing golf tomorrow morning. I need a few bucks for the weekend, so get ready to reach for your wallet."

"Hey," I laughed, "with all the strokes you'll have to give me, you're going to be handing over the dough."

I heard him chuckle and thought about how much fun it was going to be to play the next morning with my son. Tom would be lining my shots up on the course. If I were able to see, we wouldn't be playing the game on such an intimate level. With all of my senses open to the night, I thought how lucky I was to feel so positive about what it meant to be blind. I had learned how to turn this seeming disadvantage into an ultimate advantage.

At that moment, I couldn't think of one circumstance in which a disadvantage could not be turned into something positive. Disability can become ability, and inner beauty can shine out from a physical deformity. The adversity of any life circumstance can force us to dig deep and find an inner core of strength that allows us to become better people than we thought possible. The seeming disadvantage of blindness had given me the opportunity to look beyond appearances and find the true beauty that's in all of us.

As I relished the night, I realized how lucky I was to be Tom Sullivan. The phone rang, and I could tell by the animation in Patty's voice that she was talking to our daughter, Blythe, in San Diego. Blythe had grown into an extremely successful young woman, and I couldn't help but be reminded as I sat by the swimming pool that we had nearly lost her twenty-five years ago in the swimming pool at our old house.

I involuntarily shivered not from the cold but from the memory, realizing that we are forever changed when facing major turning points. I was reminded that in these moments we gain more understanding and insight into our own character than at any other time.

Blythe and I had shared so much as father and daughter, from our love of horses to skiing, our mutual appreciation for literature, and our joy experienced in good travel, good food, and good conversation. It's true, I always would have loved my daughter, but the turning point of the pool accident, carrying with it such major potential consequence, brought us far closer together.

The basic ingredient, the staple, the foundation that all of us need to build on is our self-worth. How do you feel about you? Do you doubt yourself? Do you feel unworthy or less valuable in relationships?

It's critical to believe that you are unique. You ought to stand for your own uniqueness. Without belief in your own self-worth, no other piece of the human puzzle will ever find its appropriate place.

A positive self-image does not come as a miracle from on high. It arises out of a work ethic that provides you with constant proof that you are valuable. Self-image is tested in the fire of your life experience, and you must be willing to fail almost as often as you succeed.

There is an inherent responsibility that goes with your quest for success. You must take personal responsibility for individual daily effort—the acronym PRIDE (see Life Secret #5)—proving to the world that you are competent and confident in your ongoing effort to contribute to the human family. And about that family? I'm not embarrassed to acknowledge that I love people. All of you who read this book and everyone I've had the privilege of knowing offer me personal interaction that is usually stimulating and informative and, at the least, a learning experience. People are the most interesting inhabitants of the world: No two of us are the same, and no two of us present to each other the same sort of challenges and opportunities to grow together.

All of the elements that go into our personal makeup are put together in diverse and wonderful ways. I may never see a rainbow, but the differences found in people allow me to understand the true colors of the heart, and I am enriched by the complete people experience.

Patty was playing music from our son's new album, a piece called "Grown for the Groove." As I listened, I realized that was exactly how he felt about his art. He was not only sure he had found his purpose, but he was also purposeful in his efforts.

Without purpose, we are rudderless ships adrift on a lonely and treacherous sea. We must seek out purpose without being afraid to try and fail. History is replete with stories about human beings who found purpose at different points in their lives. There's no set age or time, place or situation that any of us can point to when the element of purpose is mixed into our formula; but to be purposeless is certainly the toughest burden any of us can bear.

If you are proud of yourself and appreciate the people with whom you interact, allowing you to fulfill your purpose, you are ready to add the fuel of your individual passions. Although sometimes my passions overwhelm my judgment, I am passionate about everything in my life experience, beginning with my family and friends, followed by my work, hobbies, causes, and the environment.

How could life be meaningful to any of us if we did not pursue it passionately? I could feel myself smile in the darkness as I realized how many passions I had actually undertaken, dragging Patty and the family along as I allowed all of my hopes and dreams to take flight.

Something stirred in the bushes at the far end of the yard, and my dog, Partner, leaped from the ground where he'd been resting, racing in hot pursuit of whatever creature had disturbed the peace of the moment. I thought about how fearless my friend was. I had no doubt that either within his work as a guide dog or in the defense of his master, Partner would lay his life down for the person he loved. Ah, to be that fearless, I thought. We are all so prone to be fearful about so many circumstances that affect us. Aside from my own personal phobias, I knew that my fear factor was one of failure, and that I had often not been willing to attempt to succeed because of an overriding concern that I would not be good enough to achieve my goals.

The process of living has to be about our willingness to jump into the fray, to get our feet wet, to take a chance. They used to say on ABC's *Wide World of Sports*, "to go where no man has gone before," and "to experience the joy of victory along with the agony of defeat." At fifty-five, I understood that I would continue to place my feet in the fire and accept the challenges presented to me, because only through challenge do we enjoy the game. Thinking back on the many roads I had taken, I realized that opportunity had only knocked when challenge first presented itself, and it was challenge that had always led me to the winner's circle.

It really was true, I thought: the greater the risk, the greater the reward. I didn't believe it meant that we should all be throwing ourselves into an idea just because it popped into our heads. I had learned that preparation counted as much as perseverance and that risk and reward must be well balanced.

In the soft comfort of the summer night, I understood the bottom line was that we must be willing to take a leap of faith. This leap goes beyond the idea of risk/reward because it literally is a leap into the space we call the unknown. Risk/reward becomes our operational concept, but a leap of faith is necessary if we are to turn our dreams into realities.

But what about the brick-on-brick approach necessary to build the root system, the bulwarks, the fundamental foundations of a structured life? They take shape if we are able to create a life plan variable enough to cope with change yet definite enough to keep us on a direct path to our goals.

I smiled in the darkness, realizing that making a life plan was something I was just beginning to learn how to do to. I had always flown by the seat of my pants, and, if I was honest with myself, completely enjoyed the ride. Some people need more structure than others—that's a decision each of us has to make—but no one can achieve the desired result without some fixed commitment to a life plan.

As I luxuriated under the stars, my instinct told me that I had found the right balance between the structure of a life plan and the wish list that all of us must embrace in the pursuit of our dreams. The wind had shifted slightly, allowing me to hear two of my favorite sounds: the foghorn announcing safe harbor to ships, and the bell buoy, with the ebb and flow, to and fro of the mighty Pacific. I was part of the world—a small part of the wheel but content with the role I had been given. I had performed on life's stage in numerous ways, all of them helping me to grow and become the best Tom Sullivan possible. As the fog prompted a late evening chill in the air and I thought about going inside, I knew that life was a miracle of creation.

I have experienced the world in different ways from most of you, but in this book I fervently hope that you've come to understand how much of what I've experienced is available if you just open your hearts and minds to all that blesses us and surrounds us.

We have an unlimited capacity to drink from the cup of the possible without ever having to accept the impossible.

I see the human spirit as a light that illuminates all of the potential that makes each of us special. I have not arrived at this balanced sense of self easily. It has come through trial and error, and learning to cope with human misfortune.

So why am I so positive? Because I believe in the fantastic experience of being alive. There's so much to do, so much to sense, so much to be, so much to feel, so much to know, and so many to love.

As I see it, life will only get better if we continue to apply all of the lessons we learn, appreciate, treasure, and express along the way.

INDEX

215